The MYSTERY of GOD'S WILL

Insight for Living
Bible Study Guide

From the Bible-teaching ministry of

CHARLES R. SWINDOLL

INSIGHT FOR LIVING

Chuck graduated in 1963 from Dallas Theological Seminary, where he now serves as the school's fourth president, helping to prepare a new generation of men and women for the ministry. Chuck has served in pastorates in three states: Massachusetts, Texas, and California, including almost twenty-three years at the First Evangelical Free Church in Fullerton, California. He is currently senior pastor of Stonebriar Community Church in Frisco, Texas, north of Dallas. His sermon messages have been aired over radio since 1979 as the *Insight for Living* broadcast. A best-selling author, Chuck has written numerous books and booklets on many subjects.

Based on the outlines and transcripts of Charles R. Swindoll's sermons, the study guide text was developed and written by the Educational Ministries Department at Insight for Living.

Editor in Chief:
Cynthia Swindoll

Study Guide Writer:
Jason Shepherd

Senior Editor and Assistant Writer:
Wendy Peterson

Assistant Editor:
Glenda Schlahta

Editors:
Christina Grimstad
Karla Lenderink

Copy Editor:
Marco Salazar

Rights and Permissions:
Julie Meredith

Text Designer:
Gary Lett

Graphic System Administrator:
Bob Haskins

Director, Communications Division:
John Norton

Print Production Manager:
Don Bernstein

Project Coordinator:
Jennifer Hubbard

Printer:
Sinclair Printing Company

Unless otherwise identified, all Scripture references are from the New American Standard Bible, updated edition, copyright © The Lockman Foundation 1960, 1962, 1963, 1968, 1971, 1972, 1973, 1975, 1977, 1995. Used by permission. Scripture taken from the Holy Bible, New International Version, Copyright © 1973, 1978, 1984 International Bible Society, used by permission of Zondervan Bible Publishers [NIV]. The other translations cited are *The Message* and the *King James Version* of the Bible [KJV].

ISBN 1-57972-334-9

Cover design by permission of the Puckett Group
Cover image by permission of Sharpshooters
Printed in the United States of America.

CONTENTS

INTRODUCTION

I don't think I've ever met any Christian who hasn't struggled with the desire to know God's will. The problem is, many people hold the mistaken idea that if they just somehow find that single and simple plan God has for them, they will be effortlessly swept through life.

It's not like that.

As Christians, we know whatever happens to us happens for God's glory and for our good. But in this process toward maturity, it is easy to forget that we must journey through difficulties and struggles as He prepares us for what is best. Probably the single most misunderstood factor of discovering God's will is the thought, "If I do this, the struggles end, the questions are over, the answers come, and I live happily ever after." But that's fantasy thinking, which turns God into a tooth fairy.

Reality tells us that bad things happen to those who are sincere followers of Christ. The unexpected can waylay the best laid plans of the godly. God doesn't usually act the way we thought He would. What He does or doesn't do often makes no earthly sense. That leaves us confused and troubled about what we should do next, what life is all about . . . and what God is really like. In a word, it's a mystery.

I designed this series with that word in mind. My great hope is to clarify some confusion and put struggling saints at ease. One thing is for sure: this is not going to be an airtight, no-more-questions-to-ask sort of study, so don't expect that. I want to challenge you, first and foremost, to think theologically . . . and then accept that sometimes the best we can do is stop asking *why* and live in the midst of the mystery of an inscrutable God, who isn't obligated to explain his unfathomable ways.

Chuck Swindoll

PUTTING TRUTH
INTO ACTION

K nowledge apart from application falls short of God's desire for His children. He wants us to apply what we learn so that we will change and grow. This study guide was prepared with these goals in mind. As you go through the following pages, we hope your desire to discover biblical truth will grow as your understanding of God's Word increases, and that you will be encouraged to apply what you've learned.

To assist you in your study, we've included a section called Living Insights at the end of each lesson. These exercises will challenge you to study further and to think of specific ways to put your discoveries into action.

In this edition, we've added Questions for Group Discussion, which are formulated to get your group talking about the key issues in each lesson.

There are many ways to use this guide—in personal devotions, group studies, discussions with friends and family, and Sunday school classes. And, of course, it's an ideal study aid when you're listening to its corresponding *Insight for Living* radio series.

To benefit most from this study guide, we would encourage you to consider it a spiritual journal. That's why we've included space in the Living Insights for recording your thoughts and discoveries. We hope you'll return to those sections often for review and encouragement as you continue to grow in your walk with Christ.

Insight for Living

The
MYSTERY
of
GOD'S
WILL

PART ONE

The BUFFETINGS of GOD'S WILL

Buffeting is not a word we usually associate with the subject of God's will. The word brings to mind waves splintering a ship's hull, winds pummeling trees until they bow and finally break, a gang beating a helpless victim senseless. How could these hurt-filled images possibly have anything to do with something as hope-filled as God's will?

The truth is, most of the men and women in Scripture experienced buffeting as they followed God's will. Moses was constantly buffeted by the complaints and rebellions of the Israelites. David was buffeted by Saul's monomaniacal pursuit. And God's own prophets were ridiculed, imprisoned, threatened with death, and murdered.

The ultimate example is Jesus, whose steps varied not one footfall from the Father's way; yet where did that way lead Him? Through the violent storm on the Sea of Galilee, the brutal beating at the hands of the Roman soldiers, and the Cross itself.

Though Christians don't talk much about this painful side of God's will, most of us have experienced it in one form or another: illness, abandonment, betrayal, unanswered prayer, dead ends, exhausting delays, loss of a loved one, financial distress. The spiritual struggles and doubts that accompany these hardships are often the most difficult part to bear. We know that God is in all this—but exactly how His will and our buffeting fit together, well, that's the mystery in which many of us live every day. And it is the mystery into which we launch our study.

Chapter 1

FOUNDATIONAL PRINCIPLES ABOUT GOD'S WILL
Selected Scriptures

Have you ever driven your car in fog? A few feet of asphalt in front of your bumper is all you can see. As you reduce your speed to a crawl, strange, shadowy shapes emerge from the mist. A trunkless tree limb appears overhead then disappears as you pass by. A parked car reveals itself then vanishes. A yellow construction light blinks a warning then fades into the murk.

Driving in fog can be unsettling and disorienting. You can't see far enough ahead to know where you're going or what you might run into. You can't even see the other drivers on the road.

The journey of life can be equally disorienting. Sometimes a fog bank of uncertainty settles on us, and we have trouble knowing where we should go, what we should do, or how we should interpret the relationships and events in our lives.

You may be going through one of those mist-shrouded times right now, and perhaps this is what draws you to study God's will. As we explore this topic together, we hope you will gain some clarity and confidence in God's direction for you. However, one of the main truths we should emphasize at the outset is this: sometimes the fog *is* God's will.

Recognizing and accepting life's lack of clarity has been a clarifying experience for Chuck Swindoll, who writes in the introduction of his book *The Mystery of God's Will:*

> So much of the confusion we encounter in life
> goes back to our not understanding God and how

This chapter correlates to the first two chapters in the book "A Process and a Puzzle" and "God Decrees . . . God Permits." Charles R. Swindoll, *The Mystery of God's Will* (Nashville, Tenn.: Word Publishing, 1999).

He does His inscrutable work in our lives. In recent years, I have struggled with many of what I am calling "mysteries" in my own life. As a result, I have come to a new understanding of God's will. In the past, I often viewed the Christian life, or even just life in general, as a matter of getting from here to there . . . from point A to point B. I now believe that God's will for us in this life is not some black-and-white objective equation designed to take us to an appointed destination here on earth as much as it is about the journey itself.[1]

God's will is not so much about results (the "destination") as it is about process (the "journey"). It's not so much about choosing jobs and deciding where to live, although those are very significant decisions. More often, it's about building faith as we grapple with God's mysterious ways.

God's Ways and Our Ways

Unfathomable. That's the word the patriarch Job used to describe the mysterious ways of God, who rules His creation with a mighty hand:

"It is God who removes the mountains, they know
    not how,
When He overturns them in His anger;
Who shakes the earth out of its place,
And its pillars tremble;
Who commands the sun not to shine,
And sets a seal upon the stars;
Who alone stretches out the heavens
And tramples down the waves of the sea;
Who makes the Bear, Orion and the Pleiades,
And the chambers of the south;
Who does great things, *unfathomable*,
And wondrous works without number."
(Job 9:5–10, emphasis added)

---

1. Charles R. Swindoll, *The Mystery of God's Will: What Does He Want for Me?* (Nashville, Tenn.: Word Publishing, 1999), p. ix.

According to the NASB marginal note, the word *unfathomable* literally means "until there is no searching out." We could trace God's hand through the ages, recording His works in enough books to fill the whole world, and still our search to understand Him would have only begun. There is no searching out God! No one can say of His plan, "I've got it! I've figured it out!"

One reason for the mystery is that God thinks and operates on a different plane than we do.

"For My thoughts are not your thoughts,
Nor are your ways My ways," declares the Lord.
"For as the heavens are higher than the earth,
So are My ways higher than your ways
And My thoughts than your thoughts."
(Isa. 55:8–9)

As finite humans, we simply cannot comprehend the mind of an infinite God. Paul writes,

Oh, the depth of the riches both of the wisdom and knowledge of God! How unsearchable are His judgments and unfathomable His ways! For who has known the mind of the Lord, or who became His counselor? (Rom. 11:33–34)

Like astronomers studying the night sky, we peer into the vastness of God, searching His mind for reasons, motives, and intentions. An only child dies, and we cry out, "God, what are You doing?" A father or mother abandons the family, and we beg God to help us make some sense of it. A tragedy strikes, such as an illness, an accident, or a natural disaster, and we look up for answers. But even our best theological telescopes are too weak to reveal the farthest reaches of God's purposes. No matter how educated we are, no matter how long we've walked with God, no matter how perceptive we are, we may never completely understand why He does what He does.

Our limitations ultimately lead us into the realm of faith and confront us with some soul-probing questions. Can we trust a God we don't completely understand? Can we accept the fact that some parts of the picture will always be missing? Can we embrace God's will even though we can't fully grasp it?

Two Facets of God's Will

While we strain to see God through a telescope, God sees us in microscopic detail from beginning to end, conception to the grave. According to the psalmist, He knows "when I sit down and when I rise up," and He even knows my thoughts and hears my words before I say them (Ps. 139:1–2, 4). He is "intimately acquainted with all my ways" (v. 3). And in His book, He has written all "the days that were ordained for me" (v. 16b).

We can view this divinely detailed plan of our lives from two seemingly opposite angles. The first is the angle of God's sovereignty; the second, human free will.

The Decretive Will of God

As the sovereign ruler of the universe, God decrees and determines everything that happens in His world. This is sometimes called the "decretive" or "determined" will of God. God is at the helm of His creation. Not fate, not chance, not some impersonal force of nature but the Lord alone is in full command of our life's course. This is the message the Lord gave Isaiah:

> "That men may know from the rising to the
>   setting of the sun
> That there is no one besides Me.
> I am the Lord, and there is no other,
> The One forming light and creating darkness,
> Causing well-being and creating calamity;
> I am the Lord who does all these." (Isa. 45:6–7)

This, too, is mystery. How can the hand of a loving God chart a course for us that includes pain and calamity? It is incomprehensible. Yet, if it were not so, God would not be God. He would be some benevolent but powerless monarch who sits in heaven wringing His hands in fear that an unexpected tragedy might spoil His plan for our pleasure and comfort. No, if God is truly God, He is sovereign. And as the Sovereign, His will encompasses whatever occurs.

Having said this, we need to note that there are some things God *cannot* do. For example, He cannot and will not lie (Num. 23:19; Heb. 6:18). He cannot and does not tempt anyone to sin (James 1:13). He cannot and will not deny or contradict Himself (2 Tim. 2:13). God is eternally consistent.

We can make four statements, then, about God's decretive will. First, it is absolute. Second, it is immutable, or unchangeable. Third,

4

it is unconditional. And fourth, it is in complete harmony with His plan and His nature—that is, it never contradicts His holiness, justice, righteousness, and goodness.

This fourth point is particularly calming during rough seas. Since God is good, His plan ultimately leads toward good ends.

> And we know that God causes all things to work together for good to those who love God, to those who are called according to His purpose. (Rom. 8:28)

Satan may try to use the losses, failures, and tragedies to destroy us, but this verse reassures us that God always has the last word. Anything Satan intends for evil, God will turn into good. God sets our course, not Satan, and we can rest in His plan.

The Permissive Will of God

From the "free will" angle, we see a different perspective of God's will. God is indeed sovereign, yet under His umbrella of control, He permits choices—some of which are evil. This is called God's permissive will. Lewis Sperry Chafer brings some measure of clarity to this deeply mysterious reality.

> In respect to His permissive will, . . . God determines not to hinder the course of action which His creatures pursue; but He does determine to regulate and control the bounds and the results of such actions.[2]

Under the permissive will of God, we are accountable for our own choices. We can't blame God for our sin. The alcoholic, for instance, can't excuse his addiction by saying, "Since alcoholism is in God's decretive will, I had no choice. God made me an alcoholic." God doesn't "will" anyone to sin (see James 1:13–15). Rather, within His permissive will, He gives us the freedom to choose between righteousness and sin, and with that freedom comes responsibility for both the choice and the consequences.

God's permissive will and decretive will must always remain in perfect balance. God is not to blame for evil, but He is in control of it. God is not responsible for sin, but He is sovereign over it, and He will use even our immature, selfish, hurtful choices to accomplish His purposes.

2. Lewis Sperry Chafer, *Systematic Theology* (Dallas, Tex.: Dallas Seminary Press, 1947), vol. 1, p. 236.

How God Reveals His Will

Thankfully, not everything about God's will is a mystery. In Scripture, God reveals His will in unmistakable terms.

Scripture's Moral Road Signs

God's commands in Scripture appear like road signs, revealing the way we should go. Leslie and Bernice Flynn give us a sampling of the clear directions the Lord gives:

> Obey parents (Eph. 6:1)
> Marry a Christian (2 Cor. 6:15)
> Work at an occupation (1 Thess. 4:11–12)
> Support your family (1 Tim. 5:8)
> Give to the Lord's work and the poor (2 Cor. 8, 9; Gal. 2:10)
> Rear children by God's standards (Eph. 6:4)
> Meditate in the Scriptures (Ps. 1:2)
> Pray (1 Thess. 5:17)
> Have a joyful attitude (1 Thess. 5:16)
> Assemble for worship (Heb. 10:25)
> Proclaim Christ (Acts 1:8)
> Set proper values (Matt. 6:19–21; Col. 3:2)
> Have a spirit of gratitude (Phil. 4:6)
> Display love (1 Cor. 13)
> Accept people without prejudice (James 2:1–10)[3]

When we wonder what God's will is for us, we may not have to look any further than the pages of Scripture. The more we know God's Word, the more we will understand God's will.

The Ways God Revealed His Will in Scripture

How did God reveal His will before the Bible was completed? In those days, it was necessary for Him to use special methods to communicate His will.

First, *God spoke through miracles.* Through the miracle of the burning bush, God unveiled His plan to Moses to deliver His people from bondage (Exod. 3). In Gideon's case, it was a miracle fleece

---

3. Leslie and Bernice Flynn, *God's Will: You Can Know It* (Wheaton, Ill.: Scripture Press Publications, Victor Books, 1979), p. 26.

that confirmed God's direction (Judg. 6:36–40). Many of the miracles in Scripture served as arrows pointing out God's way.

Second, *God spoke through dreams and visions*. In a dream, Joseph learned that his brothers would one day bow to him (Gen. 37:5–11). A vision of a sheet full of nonkosher food convinced Peter to preach the gospel to Gentiles (Acts 10:9–17, 27–29).

Third, *God spoke audibly*. Young Samuel heard the voice of the Lord calling his name and giving divine directions (1 Sam. 3). Moses heard that same voice many times, and so did Noah and Abraham and the prophets.

Does God use these methods to reveal His will today? How we wish He would. When a critical decision has to be made, who hasn't laid out a fleece and prayed for a sign? Or pondered the secret meaning of a dream? Or pleaded with God to hear His voice?

Some believers claim God has spoken to them through these methods. Yet, because such methods are so subjective, there's no way of knowing whether the sign, dream, or voice is actually from God. Tragically, many have stumbled into ruin by mistaking a feeling or a coincidence as a sign from heaven.

Today God uses a much more objective and reliable source of revelation: the Bible. Now, God's Word will not tell us which career to choose, which spouse to marry, or which home to buy. But it will shape the choices we make by providing the ethics and life principles we need in order to live as Christ would have us live. So look in the Book, and let the light of Scripture be your guide through the fog.

> Your word is a lamp to my feet
> And a light to my path. (Ps. 119:105)

Living Insights

Most people come to a study of God's will for specific reasons. Some feel like they are lost in a forest of decisions, and they're looking to God for direction. Others feel disillusioned about their path in life, and they're looking to God for a better way. Still others have been wounded along their journey, and they're looking to God for a sense of purpose to their pain.

What's your reason? What do you hope to gain through your study of God's will?

_____

_____

_____

_____

Any study of God's will is essentially a theological study, a study of God. Knowing God is the fundamental first step to knowing God's will. As you review the verses in the lesson, what characteristics about God stand out to you?

_____

_____

_____

_____

What about the mysteries of God? Is it hard for you to trust Him when you don't understand Him? What makes it the most difficult for you?

_____

_____

_____

What would you like your attitude toward God and His will for your life to be?

_____

_____

_____

Let's conclude with A. W. Tozer's prayer of praise and faith from his book *The Knowledge of the Holy*. Perhaps his eloquent words will express the desire of your soul to know God and His will for you.

> O Majesty unspeakable, my soul desires to behold Thee. I cry to Thee from the dust.
>
> Yet when I inquire after Thy name it is secret. Thou art hidden in the light which no man can approach unto. What Thou art cannot be thought or uttered, for Thy glory is ineffable.
>
> Still, prophet and psalmist, apostle and saint have encouraged me to believe that I may in some measure know Thee. Therefore, I pray, whatever of Thyself Thou hast been pleased to disclose, help me to search out as treasure more precious than rubies or the merchandise of fine gold: for with Thee shall I live when the stars of the twilight are no more and the heavens have vanished away and only Thou remainest. *Amen.*[4]

 ## *Questions for Group Discussion*

1. Share with the group your reasons for studying God's will and what you hope to gain from this study.

2. What does Chuck mean when he says, "In the past, I often viewed the Christian life, or even just life in general, as a matter of getting from here to there . . . from point A to point B"? Have you thought that way too? How has that affected your approach to knowing God's will?

3. How does thinking of the Christian life as a process or a journey change your perception of God's will?

4. How much room is there in your Christian faith for mystery?

5. What's your understanding of God's "decretive will" and His "permissive will"?

6. What scriptural truth from the lesson can you carry with you this week?

---

4. A. W. Tozer, *The Knowledge of the Holy* (New York, N.Y.: Harper and Row, Publishers, 1961), p. 20.

Chapter 2

MOVING FROM THEORY TO REALITY

Selected Scriptures

Just as a sturdy house needs a solid foundation, so our understanding of God's will needs a solid doctrinal foundation. In the previous chapter, we set in place two important cornerstones of truth: God's decretive will and God's permissive will. The Lord determines the course of our lives; yet within His sovereign plan, He allows freewill choices—the consequences of which we experience every day. God decrees, and God permits.

In this chapter, we'll build on that doctrinal groundwork with the concept of *God's desired will*. God's will for us includes the things He wants or wishes will happen in our lives. Jesus expressed the desired will of God when His heart burst with compassion for His people:

> "Jerusalem, Jerusalem, who kills the prophets and stones those who are sent to her! How often I wanted to gather your children together, the way a hen gathers her chicks under her wings, and you were unwilling." (Matt. 23:37)

Jesus longed for His people to shelter themselves under the wings of His salvation, but they turned away. Peter echoed Jesus' thoughts in regard to God's universal offer of salvation:

> The Lord is not slow about His promise, as some count slowness, but is patient toward you, not wishing for any to perish but for all to come to repentance. (2 Pet. 3:9)

God knows that not everyone will accept His offer. Those who reject Christ do so against His wishes and according to their own free will.

Unlike God's decretive will, God's desired will can be resisted or ignored—to our peril. So it is vital that we tune our ears daily

---

Portions of this chapter have been adapted from "Clearing the Hurdle of Confusion," from the study guide, *Clearing the High Hurdles*, coauthored by Bryce Klabunde, from the Bible-teaching ministry of Charles R. Swindoll (Anaheim, Calif.: Insight for Living, 1995).

to the quiet longings God has for us. This is not a theoretical exercise; this is day-to-day reality. What does God will for me today, this hour, this moment? This is the question we must ponder.

Biblical Examples of Sensitivity to God's Will

Many of the men and women of Scripture were very much aware of God's desires for them. Let's take a brief survey of some Old and New Testament people who were sensitive to God's will.

In the Old Testament

David saw himself as a student in God's classroom, eager to learn and obey. He prayed to the Lord, "Teach me to do Your will, For You are my God; Let Your good Spirit lead me on level ground" (Ps. 143:10).

Solomon warned his fellow travelers along life's journey, "Do not be wise in your own eyes; Fear the Lord and turn away from evil" (Prov. 3:7). The way that appears smooth may turn out to be full of pitfalls. God alone knows which direction is best, and the truly wise person takes Solomon's advice:

> Trust in the Lord with all your heart
> And do not lean on your own understanding.
> In all your ways acknowledge Him,
> And He will make your paths straight. (vv. 5–6)

From Israel's kings we turn to the prophets, who were (with the exception of Jonah) as attentive to God's will as musicians to the maestro's baton. The often-appearing phrase, "The word of the Lord came to . . . ," is like a rhythmic downbeat in the prophetic books that releases the music of God's will in their lives.

In the New Testament

The opening pages of the New Testament unveil the long-awaited Messiah, who epitomizes sensitivity to God's will. For Jesus, fulfilling the Father's plan was as important as life itself, and as the second member of the Godhead, He demonstrated perfect submission to the Father:

> Jesus said to them, "My food is to do the will of Him who sent Me and to accomplish His work." (John 4:34)

> "I can do nothing on My own initiative. As I hear, I judge; and My judgment is just, because I do

not seek My own will, but the will of Him who sent Me." (5:30)

Because of Jesus' sensitivity and submission to God's will, we reap the blessing of eternal life:

> "For I have come down from heaven, not to do My own will, but the will of Him who sent Me. This is the will of Him who sent Me, that of all that He has given Me I lose nothing, but raise it up on the last day. For this is the will of My Father, that everyone who beholds the Son and believes in Him will have eternal life, and I Myself will raise him up on the last day." (6:38–40; see also Heb. 5:5–9)

Following Jesus' example was Paul, who often left the door open on his ministry plans with a phrase like "if the Lord wills" (see Acts 18:21; Rom. 1:10; 15:32; 1 Cor. 4:19; 16:7). And James admonished those who attempt to live by their own will:

> Come now, you who say, "Today or tomorrow we will go to such and such a city, and spend a year there and engage in business and make a profit." Yet you do not know what your life will be like tomorrow. You are just a vapor that appears for a little while and then vanishes away. Instead, you ought to say, "If the Lord wills, we will live and also do this or that." (James 4:13–15)

James is right. Only the Lord knows what tomorrow holds, so we ought to seek to do only His will today. But how does God reveal His will to us? Let's take a closer look at this important question.

Becoming Aware of God's Will Today

As we delve into this issue, we need to keep in mind six conditions for accurately knowing God's will.

1. We must place our faith in Christ as Savior, because spiritual sensitivity and discernment are "family truths" that can only be applied to members of God's family.

2. We are helped greatly by physical and emotional health, because the lack of them can fog our ability to interpret God's will.

12

3. We need a good measure of common sense.

4. We must have a true desire to know God's will (see John 7:17).

5. We need the patience to pray and wait.

6. We must cultivate a willingness to give up personal comforts, which God may call us to do (see Acts 20:22–24).

With these established, let's dig into the question: How does God lead us into His will today?

Through His Written Word

God's Word is the brightest beacon showing the way:

The unfolding of Your words gives light;
It gives understanding to the simple.
(Ps. 119:130; see also v. 105)

For the commandment is a lamp and the teaching
is light,
And reproofs for discipline are the way of life.
(Prov. 6:23)

In Scripture God gives us precepts and principles, specific instructions and general directions. J. Grant Howard, in his book *Knowing God's Will—and Doing It!*, explains,

The sign that reads "SPEED LIMIT 25 MPH" is a precept. The sign that reads "DRIVE CAREFULLY" is a principle.[1]

Precepts are black-and-white, with no grays in between. They are finely tuned commands that remove the guesswork. For example, "Do not associate with a gossip" (Prov. 20:19b); "Do not lie to one another" (Col. 3:9a); "This is the will of God . . . that you abstain from sexual immorality" (1 Thess. 4:3).

Principles, on the other hand, are like umbrellas, covering a variety of situations. For instance, Paul says,

All things are lawful for me, but not all things are profitable. All things are lawful for me, but I will not be mastered by anything. (1 Cor. 6:12)

---

1. J. Grant Howard Jr., *Knowing God's Will—and Doing It!* (Grand Rapids, Mich.: Zondervan Publishing House, 1976), p. 28.

Can you identify a principle from this verse? To what specific situations can you apply that principle? The answers require sound interpretation and mature thinking. Try to grasp Paul's thought flow and understand how his readers perceived his words. Then your application will better reflect Paul's—and the Holy Spirit's—true meaning.

Beware of the flip-and-point method of finding God's will—blindly flipping open your Bible and pointing to a verse to find a special message from God. A doctor would never use such a method with a medical encyclopedia to prescribe treatment, and neither should we rely on haphazard Bible interpretation to determine the course of our lives.

In most situations, biblical precepts and principles will illumine the direction God wants us to take. Sometimes, though, our choices will not fall within clear scriptural boundaries. Then how does God lead us?

Through the Inner Prompting of the Holy Spirit

Paul wrote in Philippians 2:

> So then, my beloved, just as you have always obeyed, not as in my presence only, but now much more in my absence, work out your salvation with fear and trembling; for it is God who is at work in you, both to will and to work for His good pleasure. (vv. 12–13)

Working out our salvation simply means to live out our Christianity, and we do this "with fear and trembling," which essentially means having a sensitive heart. This sensitivity produces a deep desire *not* to miss God's direction; so we stay keenly alert to His working inside us.

Jude is a good example of a believer with a keen spiritual awareness of God's leading. He intended to write his epistle on the subject of salvation but changed direction because of a certain inner prompting. Listen to how he put it:

> Beloved, while I was making every effort to write you about our common salvation, *I felt the necessity* to write to you appealing that you contend earnestly for the faith which was once for all handed down to the saints. (Jude 3, emphasis added)

Like Jude, when we feel the Master's hand and hear His voice in our inner chambers, we should follow Him. How else does the Lord lead us?

Through the Counsel of Wise, Qualified, Trustworthy People

Just as a quarterback calls a time-out to consult the coach about the next play, so we need to seek the insight of objective, experienced people—particularly in those fourth-and-one situations when you don't know whether to punt or plow ahead. As the proverb says,

> Without consultation, plans are frustrated,
> But with many counselors they succeed.
> (Prov. 15:22)

We can see this truth in action in Moses' life when Jethro, his father-in-law, advised him about how to better manage the crowds coming to him (Exod. 18:13–27). Today, those in business regularly hire consultants to help them succeed. Schools do too. Seeking counsel, then, is simply a smart thing to do.

After we've made our decision, how do we know we've chosen God's way?

Through the Assurance of Peace

Whether things work out happily or trouble intensifies, we will have inner peace when we are doing God's will. Paul says,

> Be anxious for nothing, but in everything by prayer and supplication with thanksgiving let your requests be made known to God. And the peace of God, which surpasses all comprehension, will guard your hearts and your minds in Christ Jesus. (Phil. 4:6–7; see also Rom. 8:6)

His settled assurance in our hearts is an important barometer, letting us know if we've made the right choice.

Sometimes that inner peace emerges as a deep sense of satisfaction. No other job, for example, would be as fulfilling—even one that paid a higher salary. No other place to live would feel like home. You know you're right where you belong.

Finally, and perhaps most importantly, you'll know your choices are in God's will when they glorify Him—when they reflect His holiness, His righteousness, His purity, His kindness, His truth, His love, His life. As Jesus told us,

"Let your light shine before men in such a way that they may see your good works, and glorify your Father who is in heaven." (Matt. 5:16)

There's no higher measure than this.

Living Insights

Are you trying to discover God's will in a specific area of your life? Take a moment to jot down the nature of the decision confronting you.

_____

_____

_____

Think of the four principles on becoming aware of God's will as lamps that can illumine your path. Let's look at your decision in the light of each principle. First, what guidance is God's Word giving you?

_____

_____

_____

What direction do you sense from the inner prompting of the Holy Spirit?

_____

_____

_____

What advice have qualified counselors offered?

_____

_____

_____

What direction seems to bring the most peace, satisfaction, and glory to God?

_____

_____

_____

Are you seeing your path a little clearer? Hope so! In the next chapter, we'll look at a few concepts that will help you put your new insight into action.

 ## Questions for Group Discussion

1. Did your parents have a "desired will" for your life? How did they communicate their wants and wishes for you? How did you respond?

2. What are some similarities and differences between your parents' desired will and God's desired will?

3. How clearly has God communicated His desired will to you through the years? Can you give examples of some of the ways?

4. If you feel comfortable, tell the group about the decision you listed in the Living Insights. In what ways do the four principles from the lesson offer you guidance?

5. If you are struggling to figure out God's desired will, what hope does Psalm 32:8 give you?

6. What can you do this week to become more sensitive to God's will for you?

Chapter 3

FLESHING OUT
THE WILL OF GOD

Hebrews 11:4–10

So far in our study of God's will, we've focused on discovery. What is God's will and how can I know it for my life? This phase is a lot like mapping an ocean voyage. We find out God's destination for our lives, then we try our best to chart a course we think will take us there. In this chapter, we'll focus on the doing phase when we weigh anchor, hoist the sails, and shove off from our home port.

The process sounds simple enough. Discover God's will, then do it.

But what sounds simple isn't always easy. Doing God's will involves an element of (here's our word again) *mystery*. We may think we know God's plan, but we can never be certain what lies ahead. Unforeseen storms may drive us off course or threaten to sink us. Midway to our destination, God may reveal a change of direction and lead us somewhere unfamiliar. In reality, we can no more map out our lives than we can know the future. God alone knows the course our lives will take.

Doing God's will, then, is first an act of bending our will to His and yielding our destiny to Him. If we don't, we may never leave the security of home. Discovering God's will requires sensitivity, but doing it requires surrender—and surrender rarely comes without a struggle.

Two Challenges of Fleshing Out God's Will

In their book *Experiencing God*, Henry Blackaby and Claude King say the struggle of surrendering ourselves to God begins at a decision point they call the "crisis of belief." This is the first challenge of fleshing out God's will: Can we trust God to accomplish through us what we can't accomplish ourselves? According to Blackaby and King, our decision requires *faith*—believing that God is who He says He is and will do what He says He will do. That faith produces *action*—stepping into the unknown.[1]

---

1. Henry T. Blackaby and Claude V. King, *Experiencing God* (Nashville, Tenn.: Broadman and Holman Publishers, 1994), pp. 133, 149.

Our action leads to the second challenge: "major adjustments." Blackaby and King point to Peter as an example of someone who faced this challenge when God called him to preach the gospel to Cornelius, a Gentile (see Acts 10). As a Jew who considered Gentiles unclean, Peter had to adjust his perception and his behavior toward Gentiles in order to do God's will.[2] That major adjustment required Peter to *release* his familiar Jewish ways and *risk* rejection and ridicule.

Are you facing a major adjustment by doing God's will? Is He leading you to release the familiar and risk the unknown? Is God asking you to put your faith into action?

One thing is certain, as Blackaby and King correctly observe, "You cannot stay where you are and go with God at the same time."[3] We can't sit on the dock and expect God to take our voyage for us. Doing God's will requires that we shove off in faith. Fortunately, the Bible supplies many examples of men and women who did just that.

Four Models of Doing God's Will

Many of these models are found in the biblical photo album of Hebrews 11, which opens with a definition of faith: "Now faith is the assurance of things hoped for, the conviction of things not seen" (v. 1). To paraphrase, *faith is trusting God when I'm unable to provide proof and obeying Him when I'm unsure of the outcome.*

What can we expect if we decide to live out that definition? The men and women listed in the chapter give us a realistic picture of some of the difficulties we might encounter. Let's examine the first four who appear in verses 4–10: Abel, Enoch, Noah, and Abraham.

Abel

By faith Abel offered to God a better sacrifice than Cain, through which he obtained the testimony that he was righteous, God testifying about his gifts, and through faith, though he is dead, he still speaks. (v. 4)

Both Cain and Abel brought sacrifices to the Lord, Cain from the fruit of the ground and Abel from his flocks (see Gen. 4:1–4a). God accepted Abel's sacrifice but not Cain's (vv. 4b–5). Why?

2. Blackaby and King, *Experiencing God*, p. 150.
3. Blackaby and King, *Experiencing God*, p. 38.

Because, according to the writer of Hebrews, Abel acted "by faith." The purity of Abel's faith illuminated the wickedness of Cain's sin-darkened heart . . . and you know the rest of the story. Rather than admit his pride and repent, Cain extinguished the light that exposed him by murdering his own brother (Gen. 4:6–8).

The point we wish to emphasize is the risk that Abel took by doing God's will. Obeying God meant offending his brother, whose heart was full of sin. His example reminds us of this painful reality: *Doing God's will may upset family members.*

Few pressures are as great as the pressure to conform to family patterns. Doing God's will may reveal a few hidden secrets and trigger family conflict, sibling turmoil, and angry words. Are we prepared to cross some inviolable family line to obey God? Though dead, Abel still speaks to us of the courage of pleasing God rather than family.

Enoch

> By faith Enoch was taken up so that he would not see death; and he was not found because God took him up; for he obtained the witness that before his being taken up he was pleasing to God. (Heb. 11:5)

The next picture of faith is Enoch, who walked with God for three hundred years until God took him at age 365 (see Gen. 5:21–24). That sounds unbelievably old, but keep in mind that Enoch's grand-father lived to age 895; his father, to age 962; and his son, to age 969. By comparison, Enoch was a young man when the Lord took him!

No one probably expected Enoch's days on earth to end so soon, yet, without warning and in an instant, God translated him from earth to heaven. The application we glean is this: *Doing God's will may lead to a surprise ending.*

Sometimes a believer's life of faithful obedience is underscored by premature death. The five missionaries who were killed by the Auca Indians in South America in the 1950s are prime examples, as well as thousands of other godly men and women whose lives ended tragically short. Why would God allow their early deaths? We may never know the reason. This is another aspect of the mystery of God's will—an aspect we must be willing to accept.

Noah

> By faith Noah, being warned by God about things not yet seen, in reverence prepared an ark for the

20

salvation of his household, by which he condemned the world, and became an heir of the righteousness which is according to faith. (Heb. 11:7)

If anyone embodies the definition of faith as "the conviction of things not seen" (v. 1), it's Noah. From the time God warned him about the coming judgment to the first drops of rain (120 years), Noah saw not one shred of evidence of an impending flood. Still, he believed it would come because he believed God. Noah lived by faith, not sight.

Can you imagine the strange looks Noah must have received from his neighbors when he began building a ship four stories tall and longer than a football field—miles from the sea? For 120 years, he hammered together his boat to the beat of jeering laughter and pounding ridicule. Yet he never lost faith.

Here's the application: *Doing God's will may invite persecution.* Just because something is God's will doesn't mean people will understand. God often calls us to stand against the tide of our times, and we should expect resistance rather than approval (see Matt. 5:10–12; John 15:18–21).

Abraham

By faith Abraham, when he was called, obeyed by going out to a place which he was to receive for an inheritance; and he went out, not knowing where he was going. By faith he lived as an alien in the land of promise, as in a foreign land, dwelling in tents with Isaac and Jacob, fellow heirs of the same promise; for he was looking for the city which has foundations, whose architect and builder is God. (Heb. 11:8–10)

Abraham left the comfort and shelter of his hometown to follow a vision God had given him of a land he had never visited and an inheritance he had never seen. He didn't even know where he was going! The call of God, however, was enough to send him on his way; the details would come later.

We want all the details first, don't we? *Before* we load the camels and sell the farm. Abraham's example teaches us that we don't have to see everything before we leave home. Here's the principle: *Doing God's will means leaving the familiar for the unknown.*

This is the "release" part of doing God's will that we discussed earlier. It's frightening to let go of the things we've come to count on to grab hold of something we're unsure of. It goes against our human nature and even our common sense. But if we intend to receive the reward of doing God's will, we must be willing to take the risk.

A Concluding Thought

We passed over a key verse in this passage to highlight it here at the end:

> And without faith it is impossible to please Him, for he who comes to God must believe that He is and that He is a rewarder of those who seek Him. (v. 6)

Faith is the brick and mortar with which we build our relationship with God. Without it, no matter how hard we work at our religious activities, we can never please Him. Yet, because we live in a world of rip-offs and broken promises, we often struggle with faith. Experience teaches us to get everything in writing and read the fine print before we take anyone at their word. Many people attach prenuptial contracts to their marriage vows because they've learned the hard way not to trust anyone, even those they love.

In spite of this atmosphere of fear and suspicion, God calls us to follow Him with outstretched arms and a trusting heart. The path ahead may appear dangerously dark, and we may tremble before what appears to be a chasm of the unknown. But as risky as it feels to step out in faith, there is no safer, no better, no more peaceful place to be than in the nucleus of God's will.

How can God's will be dangerous and safe at the same time? The answer has to do with the sovereignty of God, a theological concept we introduced at the beginning of our study. In the next chapter, we'll take a second, deeper look at this most mysterious yet most comforting truth of Scripture.

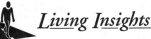 *Living Insights*

Let's pose these questions again: Are you facing a major adjustment by doing God's will? Is He leading you to release the familiar and risk the unknown? Is God asking you to put your faith into action? If so, in what specific ways?

_____

_____

_____

What fears do you have about doing God's will?

_____

_____

_____

_____

When we feel afraid to step out in faith, it often helps to meditate on God's promises in Scripture. What biblical promise encourages you the most? If you need help finding one, here are a few verses to choose from:

Psalm 23:4	Romans 8:31–39
Isaiah 41:10	Hebrews 13:5b–6

As wonderful as God's promises are, they won't give us any strength if our relationship with the Promise-giver is wobbly. Sandra Wilson, author of _Into Abba's Arms_, comments about how she has developed her walk with God and how it has strengthened her ability to trust Him:

> As I continue to listen purposefully to God and to experience more of his love for me, my love for him grows in response. And he binds my heart and will to him ever more tightly. That's how Jesus said it works: Loving hearts become obedient hearts (see John 14:15, 21).
>
> As I "descend with my mind into my heart" in times of solitude, God's presence and his promises make that journey, too. As God's _presence_ becomes real to me, God's _promises_ become real. In much of contemporary Christendom, we have emphasized the latter without the former. I know I have. . . .
>
> . . . Like many of you, I have tried living by the reality of the _promises_ without living in the reality of the _Promiser_. Yet God designed a model of

transforming change that inseparably couples the two. And we need to begin with him.[4]

If you are struggling to fully trust the Lord and do His will, perhaps the place to begin is "with Him." What can you do today to deepen your relationship with the Lord? Maybe the first journey you need to take is the inner journey of the heart into Abba's arms.

 ## Questions for Group Discussion

1. Which is more challenging for you: discovering God's will or doing it?

2. Can you recall a time when you had to make a major adjustment to follow God's will? Describe how you personally experienced the concepts of "release" and "risk."

3. Which of the four difficulties in doing God's will intimidates you the most?

4. How do you react to Chuck Swindoll's statement in *The Mystery of God's Will*: "There's no safer, no better, no more rewarding place to be than in the nucleus of His will, regardless of where that may be"?[5]

5. What advice would you give someone who was afraid to do God's will and was struggling with trusting Him?

6. How can you follow that advice this week?

4. Sandra D. Wilson, *Into Abba's Arms: Finding the Acceptance You've Always Wanted* (Wheaton, Ill.: Tyndale House Publishers, 1998), pp. 38–39.

5. Charles R. Swindoll, *The Mystery of God's Will* (Nashville, Tenn.: Word Publishing, 1999), p. 70.

Chapter 4

ANOTHER DEEP MYSTERY: GOD'S SOVEREIGNTY

Romans 11:33–36; Daniel 4:24–37; Job 38; 42

Few doctrines have caused a greater theological stir than the sovereignty of God. Within the vortex of that controversy swirls the question: "Who's in charge—me or God?" It's a question everyone asks at some time.

We like to think we're in charge of our destinies, masters of our fate. When we're sailing smoothly through life, we imagine ourselves at the helm and congratulate ourselves on our navigational skills. But then we get lost or shipwrecked, and we're frightened to realize how little control we really have.

The alternative conclusion that God is at the wheel raises its own set of problems. How can a God who loves me steer me into such treacherous waters? And the larger issue: How can an all-powerful God be in control of a world that seems to be spinning out of control?

Ironically, the answers to these questions include as much mystery as the circumstances that prompt them. The doctrine of God's sovereignty is not easy to understand. In many respects, it is beyond understanding. Where can we find the resolution and peace of mind we need?

Who's in Charge around Here?

Let's turn to two men in Scripture who can teach us about the sovereignty of God from their own experiences: one from his perch on top of the world, the other from his sorrowful place at the bottom.

Nebuchadnezzar's Boasts

Most of Daniel 4 centers on a dialogue between the prophet Daniel and King Nebuchadnezzar. The king has had a disturbing dream and tries in vain to have it interpreted. The dream baffles his wise men and mystics, so he summons Daniel. Not only does

This chapter has been adapted from "God's Sovereignty," from the study guide, Stones of Remembrance, rev. ed., coauthored by Ken Gire and Gary Matlack, from the Bible-teaching ministry of Charles R. Swindoll (Anaheim, Calif.: Insight for Living, 1994).

Daniel interpret the dream, but he talks straight to the prideful heart of the dreamer.

> "'This is the interpretation, O king, and this is the decree of the Most High, which has come upon my lord the king: that you be driven away from mankind and your dwelling place be with the beasts of the field, and you be given grass to eat like cattle and be drenched with the dew of heaven; and seven periods of time will pass over you, *until you recognize* that the Most High is ruler over the realm of mankind and bestows it on whomever He wishes. And in that it was commanded to leave the stump with the roots of the tree, your kingdom will be assured to you *after you recognize* that it is Heaven that rules.'" (Dan. 4:24–26, emphasis added)

"Until you recognize . . . after you recognize." The word *acknowledge* more precisely captures the powerful intent of the original Hebrew than the English translation *recognize*. Daniel is not urging the deluded king to merely observe but to radically accept and embrace the truth that "the Most High is ruler over the realm of mankind . . . that it is Heaven that rules."

Twelve months later, Daniel's prophecy is fulfilled when the king congratulates himself on his own greatness (vv. 29–32). True to His word, God drives Nebuchadnezzar away from human company and reduces him to an animal state—complete with hair like eagles' feathers and nails like birds' claws (v. 33).

God is in charge of the whole earth, including Babylon. Nebuchadnezzar's sovereignty is only a delegated rule, not an absolute one. Immediately afflicted with a severe mental illness, the mighty king grovels like an animal in the field for seven years. At the end of this time, the humbled king finally understands his place in God's kingdom:

> "But at the end of that period, I, Nebuchadnezzar, raised my eyes toward heaven and my reason returned to me, and I blessed the Most High and praised and honored Him who lives forever;
>
> For *His dominion* is an everlasting dominion,
> And *His kingdom* endures from generation to generation.

All the inhabitants of the earth are
    accounted as nothing,
But He does according to *His will* in the host
    of heaven
And among the inhabitants of earth;
And no one can ward off *His hand*
Or say to Him, 'What have You done?'
At that time my reason returned to me. And my
majesty and splendor were restored to me for the
glory of my kingdom, and my counselors and my no-
bles began seeking me out; so I was reestablished in
my sovereignty, and surpassing greatness was added
to me. Now I, Nebuchadnezzar, praise, exalt and
honor the King of heaven, for all *His works* are true
and *His ways* just, and He is able to humble those
who walk in pride." (vv. 34–37, emphasis added)

When Nebuchadnezzar comes to his senses, his prideful boasts
burn away like the morning mist. At last, he acknowledges who is
in charge—God. Formerly, he bragged, "'Is this not Babylon the
great, which I *myself* have built . . . by the might of *my* power
and for the glory of *my* majesty?'" (v. 30). Now the king bows his
knee and his heart to the true Sovereign: it is *His* dominion, *His*
kingdom, *His* will, *His* hand, *His* works, and *His* ways.

Job's Doubts

It's usually when our lives strike an iceberg and begin taking
on water that we ask the questions: "Is anyone at the helm of this
ship? Was anyone on the bridge looking out for icebergs?" Such
thoughts often flood our minds when calamity hits full force.

Certainly they did with Job.

In the story, Job loses everything but his life and his wife. And
to make matters worse, as he sits covered with oozing sores, he has
to endure a whirlwind of confusing, conflicting, and anything-but-
comforting counsel from his friends. How Job longs for a clear
message from God. "Why me, Lord?" Job tearfully prays.

Without realizing it, by questioning God's reasons for allowing
his suffering, Job is in effect doubting God's character and challenging His sovereignty. Beneath Job's *why* question is a larger *who*
issue that needs resolving. So, at the right moment, God breaks

His silence and reveals to Job not a list of reasons but a litany of divine deeds.

> Then the Lord answered Job out of the
> whirlwind and said,
>> "Who is this that darkens counsel
>> By words without knowledge?
>> Now gird up your loins like a man,
>> And I will ask you, and you instruct Me!
>> Where were you when I laid the foundation of
>>   the earth?
>> Tell Me, if you have understanding,
>> Who set its measurements?
>> Since you know.
>> Or who stretched the line on it?
>> On what were its bases sunk?
>> Or who laid its cornerstone . . . ?"
> (Job 38:1–6)

Throughout chapter 38 and on into 41, God continues to ply Job with questions that lead to one, indisputable conclusion: God alone is in charge and He knows what He's doing, even though Job doesn't have a clue.

In the end, Job confesses his doubts and acknowledges God as sovereign:

> Then Job answered the Lord and said,
>> "I know that You can do all things,
>> And that no purpose of Yours can be thwarted.
>> 'Who is this that hides counsel without
>>   knowledge?'
>> Therefore I have declared that which I did not
>>   understand,
>> Things too wonderful for me, which I did not
>>   know.
>> 'Hear, now, and I will speak;
>> I will ask You, and You instruct me.'
>> I have heard of You by the hearing of the ear;
>> But now my eye sees You;
>> Therefore I retract,
>> And I repent in dust and ashes." (42:1–6)

Different Stories, Same Ending

A boastful emperor dressed in jewel-studded silk, strolling marble hallways, cushioning himself on satin pillows. A bankrupt businessman dressed in rags, languishing in ashes, scraping his enflamed sores to relieve his pain. Nebuchadnezzar and Job lived worlds apart, but their paths converged at the place where all life's journeys must end: the foot of the Throne.

What do their experiences teach us? As Sovereign King, God is in control in every situation, everywhere. In golden palaces and houses of mourning. In good times and bad. Happiness and hardship. Gain and loss. Promotion and demotion. Joy and sorrow. Ecstasy and tragedy. Confusion and clarity. Illness and health. God alone is in charge, and His way (although mysterious at times) is always right.

What Does Sovereignty Mean . . . and Not Mean?

Indeed, God is *sovereign*. But what exactly does that word mean? Let's turn to the New Testament for a clarifying definition.

What Sovereignty Does Mean

Paul's doxology in Romans 11 provides us with some key information, beginning with verse 33:

> Oh, the depth of the riches both of the wisdom and knowledge of God! How unsearchable are His judgments and unfathomable His ways!

From this verse, we can formulate this definition of sovereignty: *Our all-wise, all-knowing God reigns in realms beyond our comprehension to bring about a plan beyond our ability to alter, hinder, or stop.*

Let's think about this for a moment. What characteristics must God possess in order to be sovereign? In his book *The Mystery of God's Will*, Chuck Swindoll proposes an answer:

> Whoever is sovereign must have total, clear perspective. He must see the end from the beginning. He must have no match on earth or in heaven. He must entertain no fears, no ignorance, and have no needs. He must have no limitations and always know what is best. He must never make a mistake. He most possess the ability to bring everything to a purposeful conclusion and an ultimate goal. He must

be invincible, immutable, infinite, and self-sufficient. His judgments must be unsearchable and His ways unfathomable. He must be able to create rather than invent, to direct rather than wish, to control rather than hope, to guide rather than guess, to fulfill rather than dream. Who qualifies?[1]

Certainly not you or me. Only God can fill this job description. How odd, then, that we should try to take His place or second-guess His plan. But that's what we do sometimes, don't we? In the rest of his doxology, Paul challenges us to let God be God and give Him *all* the glory:

> For who has known the mind of the Lord, or who became His counselor? Or who has first given to Him that it might be paid back to him again? For from Him and through Him and to Him are all things. To Him be the glory forever. Amen. (vv. 34–36)

Our Sovereign Lord is Master and Mover, Giver and Receiver. He is the originator, "from Him"; the enforcer, "through Him"; and the provider, "to Him."

What It Does Not Mean

But if God is in total control, where does that leave us? Some people take the doctrine of God's sovereignty to unbiblical extremes and become passive and irresponsible. God does it all, right? So why should we do anything?

It's interesting to note the commands Paul issues immediately after his doxology in Romans 11. He urges his readers to be spiritually transformed (12:1–2), exercise their spiritual gifts (vv. 6–8), develop loving relationships (vv. 9–21), and respond properly to government (13:1–7). Apparently, there is a lot for us to do.

God's sovereignty does not release us from responsibility. And that includes the responsibility for choosing our eternal destinies. Within the scope of God's reign, we have the freedom to say yes or no to Christ . . . but not the ability to change destinations once we die.

---

1. Charles R. Swindoll, *The Mystery of God's Will* (Nashville, Tenn.: Word Publishing, 1999), p. 85.

Where Will Sovereignty Lead?

Sovereignty leads us back to God's glory, for He is the ultimate end. According to 1 Corinthians 15:24–28, Christ will one day defeat all of God's enemies, including the greatest enemy—death—and deliver all things to God. And when Christ has put every rule, authority, and power in subjection to God, He will subject even Himself to the Father, so "that God may be all in all."

From beginning to end, God reigns supreme. Our happiness, our rewards, our blessings, or our relief are not central to creation's climax, but God being acknowledged as the Most High.

What Difference Does It Make?

What practical difference does God's sovereignty make? First, *God's sovereignty relieves us from anxiety.* It doesn't take away our questions, but when we release our future into His hands, we can release our worry as well.

Second, *it frees us from needing an explanation.* We don't have to know why we suffer. It is enough to know the One who knows the reasons.

Third, *it frees us from pride.* When the curtain falls and the drama of humankind is over, we may take some satisfaction in knowing we performed our best, but the ultimate praise goes to the God who wrote and directed the play. And in the end, we'll see that His plan was best after all.

> He writes in characters too grand
> For our short sight to understand;
> We catch but broken strokes, and try
> To fathom all the mystery
> Of withered hopes of death, of life,
> The endless war, the useless strife—
> But there, with larger, clearer sight,
> We shall see this—
> His way was right.
> His way was right.[2]

---

2. John Oxenham, "God's Handwriting," in *Bees in Amber* (New York, N.Y.: American Tract Society, 1913), n.p.; as quoted by Swindoll, in *The Mystery of God's Will*, pp. 92–93.

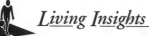 *Living Insights*

Dr. James Dobson begins his book *When God Doesn't Make Sense* with the story of a gifted medical student named Chuck Frye.[3] Chuck, a bright young Christian, entered the University of Arizona School of Medicine despite incredible odds—only 106 applicants were accepted out of 6,000. Chuck was on his way to a brilliant medical career. His bright future, however, began to dim as an unforeseen cloud settled over his life, bringing him face-to-face with the sovereignty of God.

> During that first term, Chuck was thinking about the call of God on his life. He began to feel that he should forgo high-tech medicine in some lucrative setting in favor of service on a foreign field. This eventually became his definite plan for the future. Toward the end of that first year of training, however, Chuck was not feeling well. He began experiencing a strange and persistent fatigue. He made an appointment for an examination in May and was soon diagnosed with acute leukemia. Chuck Frye was dead by November.[4]

Imagine the questions that wrung Chuck's heart when he found out he was dying. And what about his parents' struggles? How, they might have wondered, could God allow the untimely death of such a gifted and devoted young man? There are other doctors, some who profit from dishonest gain, God could have taken. Why Chuck? Why now?

Why?

This question echoes through a pain-hollowed heart. And it puts its finger on one of the troubles we have with the issue of sovereignty: *We don't know.* We don't know why, can't explain why, can't control why.

It underscores our vulnerability, forcing us to face the truth that we live in an uncertain world where bad things often happen to

3. James Dobson, *When God Doesn't Make Sense* (Wheaton, Ill.: Tyndale House Publishers, 1993), pp. 3–4.

4. Dobson, *When God Doesn't Make Sense*, p. 3.

good people. And it's hard to live with the uncertain and unknown, isn't it?

God is in control, and frankly, there is no way we can understand all that that means. It's not a simple panacea for every pain.

Yes, God is in control, but we are not. Our wholehearted belief in God's sovereignty doesn't guarantee we'll know *why*. We believe God, but we are *not* God.

So sometimes maybe the best we can do is to be honest about our vulnerable limitedness . . . and admit that we don't fully understand our sovereign, righteous, limitless Lord (see Isa. 55:8–9).

 ## Questions for Group Discussion

1. Trying to do the will of God without appreciating the sovereignty of God has caused many sincere believers to stumble. Here are just a few pitfalls we might encounter:

   - *Anger.* We might get angry at God for allowing us to suffer while doing His will.

   - *Discouragement.* We might give up following God if we feel like our success depends solely on us.

   - *Anxiety.* We might worry that God will let us down if we risk doing His will.

   - *Spiritual pride.* We might flatter ourselves in the acclaim of being such good Christians.

2. What pitfalls can you add to this list?

3. Which pitfalls are you most likely to stumble into?

4. How does acknowledging God's sovereignty help us deal with our anger? Discouragement? Anxiety? Spiritual pride?

5. In what ways did Nebuchadnezzar and Job struggle with the sovereignty of God? How did they resolve their struggle?

6. How have you struggled with the sovereignty of God? Where are you in the process of resolving your struggle, and what might help you take one step forward?

Chapter 5

READING GOD'S
MYSTERIOUS LIPS
Jeremiah 1:4–9

Young apprentices may desire to develop a trade, but without a master craftsman to guide them, how will they learn? They need a seasoned instructor to train their eyes and hands. Similarly, athletes need a coach to mold their talent, medical interns need a mentor doctor to apply their knowledge to real-life situations, and aspiring writers need an able editor to sharpen their sentences.

We all need trainers and tutors to develop our skills. But what about our life skills? Who can be our tutor for living?

Psalm 32:8 reveals the answer:

> I will instruct you and teach you in the way
>> which you should go;
> I will counsel you with My eye upon you.

The Lord Himself is our guide. He has designed for us a way which we should go—a life plan, so to speak. And He is willing to instruct, teach, and counsel us on how to follow that plan. Thankfully, though, He doesn't merely point us in the right direction and abandon us to stumble along alone. According to this verse, He keeps His eye on us, watching over us throughout our journey. Surely there is no better life guide than our God!

God, Our Guide

The Lord guided and watched over a certain young Jew named Jeremiah. Long before this prophet drew his first breath, God had already marked off his life's journey. Jeremiah records his initial encounter with his Guide:

> Now the word of the Lord came to me saying,
> "Before I formed you in the womb I knew you,
> And before you were born I consecrated you;
> I have appointed you a prophet to the nations."
> (Jer. 1:4–5)

In a voice as unmistakable as thunder on a still summer evening,

God revealed His plan to Jeremiah: "I have appointed you a prophet." Although we will never hear God calling us to be prophets, we can draw three principles from Jeremiah's call that apply to us.

"I Knew You"

The first principle emerges from the Lord's opening line to Jeremiah: "Before I formed you in the womb I knew you" (v. 5). Eugene Peterson, author of a profound book on the life of Jeremiah, *Run with the Horses*, highlights the richness of this simple truth:

> Before Jeremiah knew God, God knew Jeremiah.
> . . .
>   Jeremiah's life didn't start with Jeremiah. Jeremiah's salvation didn't start with Jeremiah. Jeremiah's truth didn't start with Jeremiah. He entered the world in which the essential parts of his existence were already ancient history.[1]

The same could be said of us—before we knew God, God knew us. Peterson unveils the application:

> This realization has a practical result: no longer do we run here and there, panicked and anxious, searching for the answers to life. Our lives are not puzzles to be figured out. Rather, we come to God, who knows us and reveals to us the truth of our lives. The fundamental mistake is to begin with ourselves and not God. God is the center from which all life develops. . . .
>   . . . If we are going to live appropriately, we must be aware that we are living in the middle of a story that was begun and will be concluded by another. And this other is God.[2]

God knows us, and more than that, He has a mission He wants us to fulfill.

1. Eugene H. Peterson, *Run with the Horses: The Quest for Life at Its Best* (Downers Grove, Ill.: InterVarsity Press, 1983), pp. 37, 38.
2. Peterson, *Run with the Horses*, p. 38.

"I Consecrated You"

The Lord also tells Jeremiah, "Before you were born I consecrated you" (v. 5). Consecrated to do what? God consecrated Jeremiah to join Him in the spiritual war that rages continually around us, as Peterson explains:

> There is evil and cruelty, unhappiness and illness. There is superstition and ignorance, brutality and pain. God is in continuous and energetic battle against all of it. God is for life and against death. God is for love and against hate. God is for hope and against despair. God is for heaven and against hell. There is no neutral ground in the universe. Every square foot of space is contested.
>
> Jeremiah, before he was born, was enlisted on God's side in this war. . . . He was already chosen as a combatant on God's side. And so are we.[3]

The implications are poignantly personal:

> I have a set-apart place that only I can fill. No one can substitute for me. No one can replace me. Before I was good for anything, God decided that I was good for what he was doing. . . .
>
> God is out to win the world in love and each person has been selected in the same way that Jeremiah was, to be set apart to do it with him. He doesn't wait to see how we turn out to decide to choose or not to choose us. Before we were born he chose us for his side—consecrated us.[4]

"I Appointed You"

Finally, God appointed Jeremiah to a specific life's calling as a prophet. Peterson says that the "word *appointed* is, literally, 'gave' (*nathan*)—I *gave* you as a prophet to the nations."[5]

Jeremiah peered over the precipice of God's will, and like a fledgling, he clung to the nest in fear. "I am a youth," he protested

---

3. Peterson, *Run with the Horses*, p. 40.

4. Peterson, *Run with the Horses*, p. 41.

5. Peterson, *Run with the Horses*, p. 41.

(v. 6), but the Lord reassured His trembling servant, "I am with you to deliver you. . . . Behold, I have put My words in your mouth." (vv. 8–9). Eventually, Jeremiah spread his wings and launched into a lifelong, turbulent adventure of faith, braving the strong and sometimes perilous currents of God's will.

God desires to give us a life vocation as well. Giving is an expression of God's loving character and an integral piece of God's created order, as Peterson writes:

> God gives himself. He also gives away everything that is. He makes no exceptions for any of us. We are given away to our families, to our neighbors, to our friends, to our enemies—to the nations. Our life is for others. That is the way creation works. Some of us try desperately to hold on to ourselves, to live for ourselves. We look so bedraggled and pathetic doing it, hanging on to the dead branch of a bank account for dear life, afraid to risk ourselves on the untried wings of giving. We don't think we can live generously because we have never tried. But the sooner we start the better, for we are going to have to give up our lives finally, and the longer we wait the less time we have for the soaring and swooping life of grace.[6]

God brings each of us to that same precipice that Jeremiah clung to. As with Jeremiah, God has known, consecrated, and appointed us for a particular purpose. However, He doesn't speak to us audibly, as He did with Jeremiah; now He communicates in silence.

How, then, do we follow His will when we can't hear His voice?

Guidelines for Reading God's Lips

Those who can't hear the voices of others learn to read the subtle movement of people's mouths. In a similar way, we can learn to read God's lips by following the subtle movement of His Spirit in Scripture and in our hearts.

As you seek God in the silence, here are five guidelines that may help you. To make it easier to remember, they begin with the first five letters of the alphabet: A-B-C-D-E.

6. Peterson. *Run with the Horses*, p. 43.

37

A—An Accepting Frame of Mind

Every day, a cacophony of sounds vies for our attention. Televisions blare; phones ring; beepers beep; bosses shout. Even our inner anxieties and stresses clamor like a houseful of noisy children, hardly giving us a moment's peace. Perceiving God's message through the din depends on our frame of mind. Are we stressed-out and distracted? Are we overbusy, overtired, and overwhelmed? If so, we will lack the focus necessary to distinguish God's guidance, and likely we will react in knee-jerk fashion to life's demands.

For this reason, we need to cultivate times of solitude and silence, through which can train ourselves to slow down. Open up. Tune in to God. In other words, we need to become sensitive and skilled in reading His lips, perceptive and patient because His plans are continually unfolding. And then we need to accept His will, whatever that might be.

B—Biblical Investigation

We've already mentioned reading Scripture to discern God's will, paying particular attention to the precepts and principles in God's Word. Here are a few other approaches in studying the Bible to find God's direction:

- Using a Bible concordance or topical reference tool, study what the Bible says about a particular word or concept, for example: *suffering* or *prayer*.

- Read a Bible passage with a friend or in a small group, and discuss together what the passage says and how it can be applied.

- Take a look at a passage from several versions of the Bible to discover different nuances of the text.

- Keep digging into Scripture, meditating on it, and memorizing verses so that the Spirit can illumine your mind with its truth.[7]

Remember, Scripture is the ultimate filter in discerning God's will. God will never lead you to do something contrary to His Word.

---

7. If you desire to learn more Bible study methods, consult the resources in the Books for Probing Further section at the end of the study guide.

C—Clarification and Conviction from the Holy Spirit

In his book *The Mystery of God's Will*, Chuck describes the way the Holy Spirit tugs on our hearts:

> This combination of God's Word and God's Spirit works within us like an inner compulsion. You're drawn, almost as if somebody has grabbed onto your clothing and is pulling you in a certain direction . . . like an inner magnet, drawing you toward that goal.[8]

Sometimes we must be content to wait for the Spirit's pull if it doesn't come right away. As David prayed,

> Make me know Your ways, O Lord;
> Teach me Your paths.
> Lead me in Your truth and teach me,
> For You are the God of my salvation;
> For You I wait all the day.
> (Ps. 25:4–5)

D—Determine If Peace Is Occurring

Another indicator of God's will is His peace that often accompanies a crucial decision (Phil. 4:6–7). The peace of Christ can act as a ruling agent in our decision-making process, like a green light at an intersection that signals, "All's clear. Proceed."

The absence of peace might be like a yellow or red light, signaling us to slow down or stop. God even guides through a spouse's level of peace. A husband, for example, may be ready to move ahead with a decision, but if his wife is churning inside about it, he is wise to keep his foot on the brake until she is ready. Decisions work out better when both husband and wife sense God's peace.

E—Expect Struggles and Surprises

Let's say you've progressed from A to D, and you are moving forward in what you believe is God's will. Suddenly, a series of problems appear like potholes in the road that jolt you out of your seat. Disappointments. Setbacks. Exhausting delays. The journey is rougher now than before you started! All these difficulties have you wondering, "Have I taken a wrong turn?"

---

8. Charles R. Swindoll, *The Mystery of God's Will* (Nashville, Tenn.: Word Publishing, 1999), p. 107.

Not necessarily. Problems aren't always signs that we've missed God's will; they could be tools that God will use to hone our faith and shape our character (see James 1:2–4). Even within the will of God, there are struggles and surprises. But we can still have peace, knowing that God is working out His plan in us.

Some Practical Advice

When Jeremiah heard God speaking to him, the main issue wasn't *knowing* God's will but *trusting* God. Perhaps, like Jeremiah, you feel God nudging you out of the nest, and you have objected with a list of reasons for why you are inadequate for the call. "I am a youth" was Jeremiah's objection. Our inadequacy, though, is the very thing that qualifies us to be successful. Why? Because success in doing God's will rests with God—otherwise it won't be *His* will.

"Can I trust the Lord to accomplish His will through me, weak as I am?" That is the question Jeremiah asked himself, and his life showed his answer, "Yes." What answer will your life show?

◢ *Living Insights*

Although we borrowed letters of the alphabet to list our points, hearing God's voice in the silence is not as easy as ABC. Our hectic schedules don't afford much time for quiet solitude. Digging into Scripture can sometimes feel like chipping into bedrock. And how do we discern the Spirit's tug from our own dreams, or the peace of Christ from our own selfish desires?

The answers aren't always clear, and that's why God's will is mysterious at times.

Recognizing the mystery relieves some of the pressure to find God's will *now*. It also eases the false guilt that says, "Something is wrong with me because I'm struggling." It's OK to admit that God's voice is difficult to hear.

We must be careful, however, not to allow our realism to decay into cynicism. We become cynical when we start doubting whether God's will exists or, if it does, that it is knowable. The end result is we fear that God has shut us off, and we give up the search for His will.

If you have come to that point of discouragement in the past, or if you are at that point right now, take heart. God isn't playing games with you. He truly wants you to know and do His will (see

Eph. 5:15–17), but perhaps part of His will is for you to develop your faith as you wander in uncertainty. This waiting period may be His will for you right now.

So don't give up. Keep working through the ABC points that we mentioned in the lesson. Even if you can't see God, God has His eye on you.

 Questions for Group Discussion

1. Who was your favorite mentor, coach, or supervisor? What qualities made this person a good guide?

2. How has God been your "life guide"?

3. Review the three principles from Jeremiah's call that Eugene Peterson highlighted. What does it mean to you that God knew you before He formed you in the womb?

4. What do you think is the difference between consecrating and appointing? How has God consecrated and appointed you?

5. Because we can't hear God's voice, we have to learn to read His lips. In what ways do the five guidelines for reading God's lips help you discern His direction for your life?

6. On which of the guidelines do you need to focus more of your attention this week?

PART TWO

The
BLESSINGS
of GOD'S WILL

"Behold, we have left everything and followed You; what then will there be for us?" (Matt. 19:27)

Peter's question to Jesus sounds a bit self-seeking, doesn't it? "So, Jesus, what's in it for us?" he seems to be asking. Yet, if we could hear Peter's voice and see his expression, we probably would perceive an attitude not of selfishness but of neediness.

Like a battle-weary soldier, Peter needs a fresh reminder of home. He needs Jesus to rekindle the fire of hope in his heart and recast his vision of the goodness and faithfulness of God. Having endured the buffetings of God's will, he needs reassurance of the blessings.

And so do we.

What are these blessings? A stock portfolio that doubles in value? Career advancements? Happy family life? Early retirement and a houseful of giggling grandchildren?

No, as much as we long for such things, they are mere shadows of the true blessings God offers those who walk with Him. "What then will there be for us?" God offers us more than we could ever dream of having in this life alone —He gives us Himself.

Chapter 6

THE MAGNIFICENT
CHESED OF GOD

Selected Scriptures

The novel *Les Misérables* was written by the highly acclaimed French author Victor Hugo in the mid-1800s. Set during the French revolution, it is the story of Jean Valjean, a man who nineteen years earlier had been sentenced to hard labor on a chain gang for stealing bread to feed his sister's starving daughter.

He's one of "the miserable," and even though he's finally paroled, he is looked on as an outcast, condemned to a life of poverty and shame.

Only the saintly bishop of Digne treats him kindly and takes him into his home to feed and shelter him. But Valjean, embittered by years of hardship, repays the bishop's kindness by stealing his silverware. Later, he is caught by the police and dragged back to the bishop to return the stolen goods before being sent back to prison.

To Valjean's astonishment, though, the bishop covers his crime, telling the police that the silverware was a gift. And along with the silverware, the bishop gives Valjean two precious candlesticks as well.

Can you imagine Valjean's relief as the police loosen his shackles and release him? Instead of the punishment he deserves, he is given freedom. Instead of a life of shame, he is offered a new beginning with the money he will gain by selling the silver. Valjean gratefully accepts the bishop's gift and dedicates his life to sharing with others the mercy he has received.

Few stories better illustrate the profound impact mercy can have on a person than *Les Misérables*. In this chapter, we will examine this life-changing ministry of God's mercy and, in particular, the relief it offers those who are laboring to do God's will.

A Definition of Mercy

Mercy isn't mere pity, understanding, or sorrow; it is divine action on behalf of offenders and victims whereby God brings relief.

This chapter has been adapted from the chapter "God's Mercy," in the study guide *Stones of Remembrance*, revised edition, coauthored by Ken Gire and Gary Matlack, from the Bible-teaching ministry of Charles R. Swindoll (Anaheim, Calif.: Insight for Living, 1994).

To give a more succinct definition: *Mercy is God's active and infinite compassion, which He demonstrates to the miserable.*

Probably no one is a greater example of mercy's relief than the apostle Paul.

> I thank Christ Jesus our Lord, who has strengthened me, because He considered me faithful, putting me into service, even though I was formerly a blasphemer and a persecutor and a violent aggressor. Yet I was shown mercy because I acted ignorantly in unbelief. (1 Tim. 1:12–13)

In the blinding light of Christ's glory on the road to Damascus, Paul saw himself for who he truly was—blasphemer, persecutor, violent aggressor. A crushing weight of guilt must have pressed down on his soul. Yet God showed mercy on him and lifted his oppressive burden. What joyous relief!

With each generation, God's mercy continues to lighten human hearts overburdened with guilt and pain; and where it lifts up, life begins anew. It did for John Newton, the eighteenth-century author of the hymn "Amazing Grace." In his self-composed epitaph he wrote:

> "John Newton, Clerk, once an Infidel and Libertine, a Servant of Slaves in Africa, was by the Mercy of our Lord and Saviour Jesus Christ, Preserved, Restored, Pardoned, and Appointed to Preach the Faith he had so long laboured to destroy."[1]

Like Paul and John Newton, we desperately needed God's mercy when we were spiritually dead in our sins (see Eph. 2:1–7, especially v. 4). And thankfully, God's ministry of mercy doesn't stop when we trust Christ for our salvation. Those mysterious, confusing times when we struggle in doing God's will can make us feel like cast members in a real-life reenactment of *Les Misérables*. It is at these trying moments when there's nothing like God's mercy to bring relief.

Some Biblical Illustrations

Turning back to the Old Testament, we find that one Hebrew word for mercy stands out—*chesed*. It's most often translated *kindness*

---

1. John Newton, as quoted by William Barclay, in *The Letters to Timothy, Titus, and Philemon*, rev. ed., The Daily Study Bible series (Philadelphia, Pa.: Westminster Press, 1975), p. 46.

or *lovingkindness*. As we trace the term through the Old Testament, we see at least five different miseries to which it brings relief.

Suffering the Consequences of Unfair Treatment

Falsely accused of raping Potiphar's wife, Joseph is imprisoned (Gen. 39). Yet in the midst of this unjust treatment, God is there as a pillow of grace in the hard circumstances upon which Joseph is forced to lay his head. The Lord doesn't right the wrong, but He helps Joseph hang on to his integrity and uses this experience as part of His bigger plan for Joseph, Egypt, and the future of the nation Israel (see 45:7; 50:20).

> But the Lord was with Joseph and extended *kindness* to him, and gave him favor in the sight of the chief jailer. The chief jailer committed to Joseph's charge all the prisoners who were in the jail; so that whatever was done there, he was responsible for it. The chief jailer did not supervise anything under Joseph's charge because the Lord was with him; and whatever he did, the Lord made to prosper. (39:21–23, emphasis added)

Enduring Grief after the Loss of a Loved One

Newly widowed, Naomi welcomed the marriages of her two sons to Orpah and Ruth. Then tragedy struck, and both sons died (Ruth 1:1–5). But Naomi's comforting words to her daughters-in-law include the assurance of God's *chesed*—His mercy and caring kindness—and the hope that He will provide them with a new life of security in another husband's arms.

> "Go, return each of you to her mother's house. May the Lord deal *kindly* with you as you have dealt with the dead and with me. May the Lord grant that you may find rest, each in the house of her husband." Then she kissed them, and they lifted up their voices and wept. (vv. 8–9, emphasis added)

Struggling with the Limitations of a Disability

Second Samuel 9 tells the story of an overlooked crippled man named Mephibosheth, the son of David's friend Jonathan and grandson of Saul, the late king of Israel. King David seeks out Mephibosheth—who trembles in his presence, for the ancient kings of the east used to annihilate the descendants of the kings they succeeded. But David allays Mephibosheth's fears with an extra-ordinary demonstration of mercy. For as God had shown David mercy in preserving his life and making him king, so now David's overflowing heart extends God's mercy to others. He tells Mephibosheth,

> "Do not fear, for I will surely show *kindness* to you for the sake of your father Jonathan, and will restore to you all the land of your grandfather Saul; and you shall eat at my table regularly." (v. 7, emphasis added)

Hurting Physically

Probably no example of prolonged physical agony stands out in the Scriptures as sharply as Job's. He was blighted with sores without and beleaguered with questions within. And in the ash heap of those unanswered questions, he sat in disgrace. In fact, "sated with disgrace" is how he described himself in Job 10:15. In the midst of overwhelming pain, a momentary glimmer of light shone through before Job's anguish darkened his mind again. He reminded the Lord,

> "'Your hands fashioned and made me altogether,
> And would You destroy me?
> Remember now, that You have made me as clay;
> And would You turn me into dust again?
> Did You not pour me out like milk
> And curdle me like cheese;
> Clothe me with skin and flesh,
> And knit me together with bones and sinews?
> You have granted me life and *lovingkindness*;
> And Your care has preserved my spirit.'"
> (vv. 8–12, emphasis added)

Commentator John E. Hartley renders *lovingkindness* as "loyal love," explaining that "with the breath of life comes God's commitment of loyal love to his new creation."[2] Job may not have been able to consistently sense God's loyal love in his affliction, just as we may struggle to, but it's there. Because our loving Lord will never leave us or forsake us (Heb. 13:5).

---

2. John E. Hartley, *The Book of Job*, The New International Commentary on the Old Testament Series (Grand Rapids, Mich.: William B. Eerdmans Publishing Co., 1988), p. 187.

Bearing the Guilt of Transgression

Probably the most miserable pain we can find ourselves in is not physical but spiritual. Psalm 32:3–5 describes the misery of those who keep their sins secret from God.

> When I kept silent about my sin, my body wasted
>   away
> Through my groaning all day long.
> For day and night Your hand was heavy upon me;
> My vitality was drained away as with the fever
>   heat of summer.
> I acknowledged my sin to You,
> And my iniquity I did not hide;
> I said, "I will confess my transgressions to the
>   Lord";
> And You forgave the guilt of my sin.

Even in our most disgraceful fall into sin, God is there to extend a merciful hand to help us up, dust us off, and get us on our feet again.

> Many are the sorrows of the wicked,
> But he who trusts in the Lord, *lovingkindness*
>   shall surround him. (v. 10, emphasis added)

In Psalm 23:6, David expresses his trust in God's *chesed:* "Surely goodness and mercy shall follow me all the days of my life" (KJV). And it is this characteristic of God that David clings to after his sin with Bathsheba:

> Be gracious to me, O God, according to Your
>   *lovingkindness;*
> According to the greatness of Your compassion
>   blot out my transgressions.
> (51:1, emphasis added)

For the fallen, the weary, the guilty, and the hurting, mercy is waiting to tenderly embrace the confessor. Mercy we can depend on to be there. Always.

Mercy at Work Theologically

Mercy is always wrapped in tenderness. In the Old Testament, when the tabernacle was built, God arranged for a box—the ark of the covenant—to be kept in the holiest place of all (see Exod. 25;

49

30:6). Set behind a thick veil, it contained the Ten Commandments and Aaron's rod. Over the tablets of stone there was a little lid exactly in the shape of the altar. Over this lid and altar were two golden angels called cherubim, one on each side, looking onto the mercy seat, or altar. This was the most intimate place in the tabernacle—the place where the blood of sacrifices was poured out century after century.

It's called the mercy seat because when the blood covers the Law, while the cherubim watch, God is satisfied and His anger is abated. How symbolic that God would choose a small lid over an ark framed by silent, golden cherubim as the place where He would commune with His people. It wasn't a place of law, it was a place of mercy.

Mercy at Work Personally

Mercy gives relief to the miserable in ways that are both intensely personal and immensely practical.

- When I am treated unfairly, God's mercy relieves my bitterness.

- When I grieve over loss, God's mercy relieves my pain and anger and denial.

- When I struggle with a disability, His mercy relieves my self-pity.

- When I endure physical pain, His mercy relieves my hopelessness.

- When I deal with sinful actions, God's mercy relieves my guilt.

How does God's mercy come to us? Most often, it comes quietly and subtly in a still, poignant moment—like the mercy that came to a certain husband in the film *Tender Mercies*.

Tender Mercies is about two opposites who marry. He is a man battling with alcohol, bitter over a lost career as a country-western musician. She's a widow whose previous husband was killed in Vietnam. She never makes enormous demands on him, never threatens him, never expects too much.

Quietly . . . graciously . . . patiently . . . with tender mercies, she trusts God to deal with her husband.

The story comes to a climax when the husband, in the throes of depression, buys a bottle and peels out in his pickup. Meanwhile, his wife waits in bed, quoting Scripture to encourage herself while he's gone. Finally, he returns, telling her, "I bought the bottle, but I poured it out. I didn't drink anything."

His life turns a corner at this point. And he goes back to the work he once loved—songwriting.

Tender mercies—that's what God uses to change and renew lives. And part of His will is for us to be like Him, to be people of mercy. To lessen our demands and increase our compassion. What a blessed world it would be if we lived more in the scope of God's mercy!

Living Insights

God's blessings come to us like streaks of sunshine breaking through storm clouds, casting a brilliant rainbow across a rain-drenched landscape. How we need to feel the warmth of God's blessings in the midst of our buffetings. And certainly there is no better blessing than God's mercy to lift our faces upward and restore our hope.

Of the five "miseries" mentioned in the lesson for which God avails His mercy, with which one do you most closely identify? Put a check mark by your choice.

❑ The bitterness of being treated unfairly

❑ The pain, anger, and denial of grief

❑ The self-pity and discouragement of a disability

❑ The hopelessness of physical pain

❑ The guilt and shame of sinful actions

A ray of God's mercy may burst through your clouds in any number of forms: the soft-spoken encouragement of a friend, the moving words of a hymn, the comforting truth of a Bible verse, an unforeseen change in circumstances, a new perspective or insight.

Would you like to take a prayerful moment right now and ask God for a burden-relieving demonstration of His mercy? We've provided space here and on the next page to pen your prayer.

_____

_____

_____

_____

_____

_____

_____

_____

_____

Now, tell the Lord that you are willing to wait for His tender mercies in His way and in His time.

 ## Questions for Group Discussion

So far in our study, we've focused on a side of God's will that is difficult to understand—*mysterious*, is our word—because of the unexpected struggles and doubts that sometimes blindside us as we follow the Lord. This chapter adds another theme: God's will to bless us in the midst of the buffeting.

1. As Christians, we use the word *blessing* in many different contexts. What are some of the ways you've used the word or heard others use it?

2. We may picture the blessings of God's will as a stream of sunlight through a stormy sky or an early spring crocus pushing its petals through a crusty layer of snow. These are God's hope-filled reminders of His presence that keep us going during difficult days. What would you say is the ultimate image of God's blessing for you?

3. The subject of this chapter is God's mercy, which we defined as "God's active and infinite compassion, which He demonstrates to the miserable." Can you think of a few ways Jesus lived out this definition in the lives He touched?

4. Perhaps you can share which of the five "miseries" you most closely identify with and how that misery has impacted your life.

5. How might Jesus touch your life with His tender mercy?

6. Close in prayer as a group, asking God to demonstrate His blessing of mercy to each of the members. In your next meeting, discuss how God answered your prayer.

Chapter 7

GOD'S MYSTERIOUS IMMUTABILITY

Lamentations 3:1–32

D oing God's will can be like dieting. In both situations, little compromises undermine our best efforts. We may start early Monday morning, determined to trim off the fat. But by Wednesday we sneak one treat and then another. By Friday, we're back to our old habits. Perhaps that's why we relate so well to the "stresser's diet."

Breakfast
1/2 grapefruit
1 piece whole-wheat toast
8 oz. skim milk

Lunch
4 oz. lean broiled chicken
1 cup steamed lima beans
1 Oreo cookie
Herb tea

Midafternoon snack
Rest of the package of Oreo cookies
Quart of rocky-road ice cream
Jar of hot-fudge sauce

Dinner
2 loaves garlic bread
Large mushroom-and-pepperoni pizza . . .
3 Milky Ways
Entire frozen cheesecake, eaten directly out of
   the freezer[1]

Oh, the impact of one Oreo cookie!

This chapter has been adapted from "God's Faithfulness," in the study guide *Stones of Remembrance*, rev. ed., coauthored by Ken Gire and Gary Matlack, from the Bible-teaching ministry of Charles R. Swindoll (Anaheim, Calif.: Insight for Living, 1994).

1. Pamela Pettler, *The Joy of Stress* (New York, N.Y.: William Morrow and Co., Quill, 1984), p. 47.

Compromises complicate our commitments—whether it's our commitment to diet or do God's will. Compromises may be funny in a ridiculous diet such as this one, but they are tragic when they bring down a life or, even worse, a nation.

One wonders when Israel made that first compromise. Maybe it was when one family first found a Canaanite idol. They didn't worship it. They just decided to toss it in the closet. No big deal. After all, it was only a wood carving. It meant nothing to them. But then one of the children discovered it, or maybe a neighbor was curious; and before they knew it, one compromise led to another, and a nation fell.

> With their silver and gold they have made idols
>   for themselves. . . .
> For they sow the wind
> And they reap the whirlwind. (Hos. 8:4b, 7a)

What may have begun as the cherishing of a little artifact ended up as a massive manufacturing effort that led the nation out of God's will and into wholesale idolatry. Benjamin Franklin, back in 1758, pictured compromise's far-reaching effects: "A little neglect may breed great mischief . . . for want of a nail the shoe was lost; for want of a shoe the horse was lost; and for want of a horse the rider was lost."[2]

Now is the time to pay attention to the nail, to take a look at those little compromises, because neglecting these details is the first step down to defeat. For when we continue doing wrong, we set in motion a downward spiral of catastrophic complications.

Regretting a People's Compromises

In 722 B.C., the Assyrians invaded the northern kingdom of Israel and took the Jews of that region into captivity. Then in 586 B.C., the Babylonian army swarmed over Jerusalem, took the southern kingdom captive, and marched the people of Judah off to Babylon. God's people were indeed swept away by the whirlwind.

The prophet Jeremiah watched this upheaval and prophesied for more than forty tearful years. In his elegy for his people, The Lamentations of Jeremiah, he recorded what he saw and felt after

---

2. Benjamin Franklin, as quoted in *Bartlett's Familiar Quotations*, 15th ed., rev. and enl., ed. Emily Morison Beck (Boston, Mass.: Little, Brown and Co., 1980), p. 347.

the fall of Judah. A *lament* is "a crying out in grief."[3] It's a wailing cry in the middle of the night. It's the sadness brought on by loss. As Jeremiah looked out on the smoking rubble of Zion, he remembered with aching heart the days when his nation was great, and he made his people's grief and shame his own.

> I am the man who has seen affliction
> Because of the rod of His wrath.
> He has driven me and made me walk
> In darkness and not in light.
> Surely against me He has turned His hand
> Repeatedly all the day. (Lam. 3:1–3)

Clearly, when we live wrongly, we begin to be afflicted. God disciplines us. Judah had deliberately, consciously, and with some sense of calculation compromised the ways of God. Now His whirlwind of judgment swept the people off their feet. And Jeremiah's affliction soon turned to desolation.

> Even when I cry out and call for help,
> He shuts out my prayer.
> He has blocked my ways with hewn stone;
> He has made my paths crooked.
> He is to me like a bear lying in wait,
> Like a lion in secret places.
> He has turned aside my ways and torn me to
> pieces;
> He has made me desolate. (vv. 8–11)

Desolate, isolated, Jeremiah felt rejected by God. Then came mockery from his own people and, with it, humiliation.

> I have become a laughingstock to all my people,
> Their mocking song all the day. (v. 14)

Compromise, affliction, desolation, humiliation, isolation. Jeremiah recorded every emotion of his great grief: he was "broken" (v. 4), "blocked" (v. 9), bitter (v. 15). And at the very bottom of his pit of despair, he experienced rejection: "My soul has been rejected from peace; I have forgotten happiness" (v. 17).

---

3. *Merriam-Webster's Collegiate Dictionary*, 10th ed., see "lament."

Like the branches of a tree in a violent storm, the prophet's spirit was bowed within him (v. 20). Yet when he looked up, he saw the character of God standing firm. The Lord doesn't sway, and that changed his perspective on the storm.

Remembering God's Faithfulness

For a brief time, the gloom lifted, and Jeremiah gained strength through hope.

> This I recall to my mind,
> Therefore I have hope. (v. 21)

Hope. The human body can live forty days without food, maybe eight days without water, only a few minutes without air. But the human spirit can't live for more than a few seconds without hope. Jeremiah had been walking through the remains of the city he loved, kicking the debris, remembering the bitterness, and grieving over why this happened. Suddenly, three shining truths about God's faithfulness dawned on his darkened heart.

> The Lord's lovingkindnesses indeed never cease.
> (v. 22a)

Note the plural form—*many* are God's lovingkindnesses, many are His mercies. We need to have this truth blazed into our brains: *The Lord's mercies never cease.*

Aren't you glad God isn't fickle? Aren't you glad that, even when you run, His mercy stays? We are the sheep of His own pasture, and His goodness and mercy follow us all the days of our lives (see Ps. 23:6). They *never* cease.

The next word of hope is found in the second part of this verse and the beginning of the following one:

> For His compassions never fail.
> They are new every morning. (Lam. 3:22b–23a)

The Lord's compassions never fail. The word *compassion* means "sympathetic consciousness of others' distress together with a desire to alleviate it."[4] In reference to God, it always includes His involvement, His grace, and His forgiveness—His helping of the

---

4. *Merriam-Webster's Collegiate Dictionary*, 10th ed., see "compassion."

helpless. Like the father of the prodigal son in Luke 15, God keeps loving all His prodigal children. And His lovingkindnesses and compassions "are new every morning." Charles Dyer expands on this thought.

> Could Judah push God so far that He would finally abandon her forever? Was God's supply of loyal love and compassion limited? Jeremiah's answer was no. . . . God offered a fresh supply of loyal love every day to His covenant people. Much like the manna in the wilderness, the supply could not be exhausted.[5]

What is God's morning message to us? The dawn itself.

It doesn't matter whether the sky is clear and bright or cloudy and rainy. He says *every morning*, not just when the sun shines. Every morning the Lord sends the message: "I'm still here. Let's go through the day together. Tomorrow we'll face tomorrow. But for today, I'm here to show you love, kindness, and compassion."

In Lamentations 3:23b, Jeremiah exulted in the Lord's goodness and burst into praise:

> Great is Your faithfulness.

No matter what we do, God is faithful—it's His nature. Even when we blow it. Even when we make stupid decisions. Even when our marriages fail or our businesses go bankrupt. Even when we slip on the path of God's will. *The Lord's faithfulness never diminishes.* It is always, always great.

Because of God's immutability, His unchanging character, His faithfulness will remain unconditional, unending, unswerving. Now there's a reason to face another day . . . and face it with hope.

> "The Lord is my portion," says my soul,
> "Therefore I have hope in Him." (v. 24)

Responding to God's Goodness

Right now, in the nearness of this present moment, trust God to remember you. He's faithful to know not only *who* you are but

---

5. Charles H. Dyer, "Lamentations," in *The Bible Knowledge Commentary*, Old Testament edition, ed. John F. Walvoord and Roy B. Zuck (Colorado Springs, Colo.: Chariot Victor Publishing, 1985), p. 1217.

where you are—where you're running from, and where you're running to. And all the while, He's dogging your heels with His untiring faithfulness. He's there and He cares. How do we trust Him? We can glean four ways from Jeremiah's words in verses 25–32.

Wait patiently. Stop running and start waiting. In verse 25, Jeremiah assures us, "The Lord is good to those who wait for Him." Trust Him to remember His goodness toward you . . . by waiting on His unchanging faithfulness.

Seek diligently. Instead of ignoring Him, start seeking Him again. Confess your wrongs, uncover your shame before Him, and come to Him on the merits of Christ. For the Lord is good "to the person who seeks Him" (v. 25b).

Sit silently. Jeremiah next offered this counsel:

> It is good that he waits silently
> For the salvation of the Lord.
> It is good for a man that he should bear
> The yoke in his youth.
> Let him sit alone and be silent
> Since He has laid it on him. (vv. 26–28)

After you've poured out your heart to God, be quiet. Try spending a day in solitude. Take a passage, a psalm, a section of Scripture that's meaningful to you, and let it speak. Say nothing; just sit quietly. Let Him talk. Let Him reassure you. Feel His arms around you. Understand the cleansing He's bringing and the freshness of His presence.

Submit willingly. When God disciplines us, our tendency is to want to stand up and defend ourselves. But Jeremiah advised just the opposite.

> Let him put his mouth in the dust,
> Perhaps there is hope.
> Let him give his cheek to the smiter;
> Let him be filled with reproach. (vv. 29–30)

This means no rationalizing, no excuses. Stop trying to get around the sinful compromises in your life. Face them submissively, willingly. If you do, verses 31–32 offer a wonderful promise of encouragement:

> For the Lord will not reject forever,
> For if He causes grief,

Then He will have compassion
According to His abundant lovingkindness.

If you wait patiently, seek God diligently, sit silently, and submit willingly, He will show you that His mercies haven't ceased, His compassions haven't failed, and His faithfulness hasn't diminished.

◆

Great is Thy faithfulness, O God my Father,
There is no shadow of turning with Thee;
Thou changest not, Thy compassions they fail not;
As Thou hast been Thou forever wilt be.

Great is Thy faithfulness!
Great is Thy faithfulness!
Morning by morning new mercies I see;
All I have needed Thy hand hath provided—
Great is Thy faithfulness, Lord, unto me![6]

 Living Insights

Southern California: Sun-baked beaches caressed by whispering waves. Towering palm trees. Windswept patios and outdoor cafés. Rugged mountains. Movie stars. And smog.

Smog. It lingers in the Los Angeles Basin like an obese ghost. Fat and lazy from an undisciplined diet of exhaust fumes, it rolls over on rare occasions to allow a glimpse of the mountains. On most days, though, one must take it by faith that the peaks are there, obscured by a slothful spirit who cares more about sleep than scenery.

Walking with God is sometimes like looking for a concealed mountain, isn't it? We know He's there, that He's faithful. But spiritual smog—bloated with emotional and physical pain, relational strain, even sin—hides Him from view. What might be hiding Him from your view right now?

_____

_____

6. Thomas O. Chisholm, "Great Is Thy Faithfulness," in *The Hymnal for Worship and Celebration* (Waco, Tex.: Word Music, 1986), no. 43.

_____

_____

_____

_____

Because we can't always see Him, we walk by faith, knowing that murky circumstances can't weaken God's faithfulness any more than smog can tear down a mountain range. A glimpse of Him would sure be nice, though, wouldn't it?

How long has it been since you asked your heavenly Father to clear away the smog and reveal Himself to you? Why don't you try that now? Don't expect all your problems to disappear, but ask God to encourage you with His presence. Take along a Scripture passage or two (Psalm 139 is a great one). Get alone. Be quiet and seek God. Love Him. Thank Him. Ask of Him. Confess to Him.

Write down what He may reveal about Himself to you. And above all, enjoy the view!

_____

_____

_____

_____

_____

_____

Questions for Group Discussion

1. What began as a minor compromise ended up as a major catastrophe for the Hebrew people. How do little sins lead us so far away from God's will? Why don't we see the dangerous consequences approaching?

2. Often accompanying the mystery of God's will is the horrifying fear that God has turned His back on us. What other explanation could there be to the confusing and painful events in life? We conclude, "God has forgotten me because, in my sin, I have

60

forgotten Him." Has this thought ever crossed your mind? If so, what were the circumstances?

3. This thought probably crossed Jeremiah's mind as he was walking and weeping through the debris of Jerusalem. The rubble at his feet and the wail of the people seemed to be clear evidence that God had abandoned His people. What reminders revived his hope? How do you think Jeremiah knew these reminders were true?

4. How do you know they are true for you?

5. What can you do this week to help restore your trust in God's faithfulness?

Chapter 8

CAN GOD'S WILL MAKE US HOLY?

Selected Scriptures

These days, the word *holy* probably doesn't top most people's lists of things they want to be. Healthy, happy, wise—yes. But holy? This word can conjure up images of robed monks singing Gregorian chants in candlelit cathedrals or grim, thin-lipped Puritans whose icy stares take a holier-than-thou attitude to new heights.

Yet the Lord commands us, "You shall be holy" (1 Pet. 1:16a). What exactly does this mean? God clarifies our idea of holiness by offering Himself as the ideal: "For I am holy" (v. 16b). Whatever true holiness is, it is bound up within the resplendent majesty and beauty of the almighty God. What a contrast to our distorted image!

What Holiness Looks Like

What does real holiness look like? The prophet Isaiah gives us a glimpse of what he saw.

> In the year of King Uzziah's death I saw the Lord sitting on a throne, lofty and exalted, with the train of His robe filling the temple. Seraphim stood above Him, each having six wings: with two he covered his face, and with two he covered his feet, and with two he flew. And one called out to another and said,
> "Holy, Holy, Holy, is the Lord of hosts,
> The whole earth is full of His glory."
> And the foundations of the thresholds trembled at the voice of him who called out, while the temple was filling with smoke. (Isa. 6:1–4)

King Uzziah, you may remember, was the only king in Israel's and Judah's history to die a leper—a judgment from God because this prideful king had flouted God's holiness (2 Chron. 26:16–21). He barged in where, as Isaiah saw, even angels tread with care.

This chapter has been adapted from "God's Holiness," in the study guide *Stones of Remembrance*, rev. ed., coauthored by Ken Gire and Gary Matlack, from the Bible-teaching ministry of Charles R. Swindoll (Anaheim, Calif.: Insight for Living, 1994).

Look at the scene: the lofty throne; the enormous train of God's robe; the magnificent voices of the angels crying out God's infinite holiness, "Holy, Holy, Holy"; the billowing smoke—these images inspire awe as well as terror. They also communicate an essential characteristic of holiness: *separation*.

God, being holy, is completely separate from all that is sinful, impure, and imperfect. We, on the other hand, can never experience sinlessness in this life because of our fallen condition. So we learn to adjust to our shame and often overlook it. As we gaze at God's majestic holiness, however, we become poignantly aware of the great gulf that separates our sinful selves from our holy God. That's why Isaiah responded as he did:

"Woe is me, for I am ruined!
Because I am a man of unclean lips,
And I live among a people of unclean lips;
For my eyes have seen the King, the Lord of
hosts." (Isa. 6:5)

Thankfully, God's glorious purity does much more than simply reveal our impurity. Through God's grace, it actually provides us with many benefits.

How Holiness Benefits Us

Let's take a look at a few of the rich treasures God's holiness offers us.

Reassurances

First, God's holiness reassures us that He is trustworthy; He is morally unable to take advantage of us, abuse us, or manipulate us. His will may seem mysterious, but it is never wrong. We can trust Him to do what is right by us at all times.

God's holiness also guarantees that He will deal honorably with us; we will never have to wonder whether His plans will backfire or work against us. His holy will is free of question.

Further, since He is holy, He is our model of perfection—He is without flaw, either hidden or exposed. He has moral wholeness. According to James, God's perfection has a particularly meaningful implication regarding temptation:

Let no one say when he is tempted, "I am being tempted by God"; for God cannot be tempted by evil, and He Himself does not tempt anyone. (James 1:13)

Since evil can't touch God, even to tempt Him, we can be certain that God's touch on our lives is entirely pure. And not only is it pure, it is purifying. After Isaiah fell to his knees, utterly despairing of his sin, God reached out to him through an angel. Isaiah recounts,

> Then one of the seraphim flew to me with a burning coal in his hand, which he had taken from the altar with tongs. He touched my mouth with it and said, "Behold, this has touched your lips; and your iniquity is taken away and your sin is forgiven." (Isa. 6:6–7)

Derek Kidner explains the rich symbolism in Isaiah's imagery.

> The *live coal* symbolizes the total significance of the altar from which it came; that the penalty of sin was paid by a substitute offered in the sinner's place. The symbol, applied to Isaiah's lips (the point at which his need was most pressing), assures him of personal forgiveness.[1]

Likewise, our faith in Christ, who is our atoning substitute, is credited to us as righteousness, allowing us to stand before God forgiven and holy (see Rom. 4:5; 2 Cor. 5:21).

Privileges

What privileges accompany our holy standing before God? First, it opens the door to fellowship with Him and with one another.

> This is the message we have heard from Him and announce to you, that God is Light, and in Him there is no darkness at all. . . . If we walk in the Light as He Himself is in the Light, we have fellowship with one another, and the blood of Jesus His Son cleanses us from all sin. (1 John 1:5, 7)

"God is Light"—this statement reveals "the 'Godness' of God

---

1. F. Derek Kidner, "Isaiah," in the *New Bible Commentary: 21st Century Edition*, 4th ed., ed. D. A. Carson, R. T. France, J. A. Motyer, and G. J. Wenham (Downers Grove, Ill.: Inter-Varsity Press, 1994), p. 638.

. . . God in his essence."[2] The image of *light* communicates God's splendor and glory, His revelation and illumination of Himself and all around Him, His guidance of us, and His purity.[3] God is absolutely pure, with not one dark thought, not one stained motive, not one shady statement or act.

Because of His provision of Christ, God gives us the opportunity to overcome the darkness of our souls and walk in the light of His holiness (v. 7). As a result, we are free from the stranglehold of sin. Without God imparting His holiness to us, we would live forever under a cloud of shame, driven by evil motives, and never be able to free ourselves from the darkness. Like Isaiah, we could only cry, "Woe is me, for I am ruined!" We'd have no hope.

But God's holy grace through the forgiveness of sins gives us the privilege of one day seeing our Lord (see Eph. 5:25b–27; Col. 1:21–22; 1 Thess. 5:23–24; Titus 3:4–7; Heb. 10:19–23; 12:14).[4]

How Holiness Is Lived Out

As excellent and vital as holiness is, it can still feel out of reach, can't it? How can holiness possibly be achieved by sinful humans?

The mysteriousness of it is magnified by two conflicting approaches. One says that we can never work hard enough, never give up enough, to achieve holiness. The other says that holiness is all up to God, that we're just passive recipients who have no involvement in the process of becoming holy people.

Neither of these is very helpful—or accurate. So let's set aside our opinions for a moment and see instead what the Holy One Himself has said in His Word.

Two Foundational Principles

Two thoughts rise to the surface when we examine holiness in the Scriptures. *First*, holiness always suggests separateness and differentness. And *second*, holiness is always connected with moral

2. Glenn W. Barker, "1 John," in *The Expositor's Bible Commentary*, gen. ed. Frank E. Gaebelein (Grand Rapids, Mich.: Zondervan Publishing House, Regency Reference Library, 1981), vol. 12, p. 309.

3. See William Barclay, *The Letters of John and Jude*, rev. ed., The Daily Study Bible Series (Philadelphia, Pa.: Westminster Press, 1976), p. 26.

4. The process of being made holy is called *sanctification* (*hagiasmos*, in Greek, which is derived from the word for holy, *hagios*). Without holiness being transferred to our account through the righteousness of God, we would have no promise of heaven.

excellence and ethical beauty. To be holy as God is holy, then, means that we separate ourselves from sin and emulate God's morality. Marianne Meye Thompson, reflecting on John's statement that "God is Light" and that our proper response is to "walk in the Light" (1 John 1:5, 7), explains that the Christian should

> shape one's whole being, all one's actions, decisions, thoughts and beliefs by the standard of the God who is light, even as a circle gives shape to empty space. It does not mean to be perfect, as God is perfect, for [John's] statements about human sinfulness (1:8, 10) do not allow such an interpretation. Rather, to *walk in the light* means to live continually guided by and committed to the God who is light. What God wants of us is that we shape our lives not by an external norm or by some arbitrary standard, but in conformity with the very character and heart of God.[5]

God, then, grants us holiness through Christ—this is our *position*, which we enter through faith; so this part is passive. However, living and growing in holiness—the *process* of our calling—is definitely active: it depends on our choices, our willingness to cooperate with the Holy Spirit. Simply put, Christ has already sanctified us (made us holy), but we are still being sanctified (becoming holy). Sanctification is both God's work and our work; a divine promise and a human process.

Both the Old and New Testaments are consistent and clear about this.

Holiness in the Old Testament

Leviticus 11 shows that we aren't merely to sit back and admire God's holiness, but we're to be actively distinct and morally pure as He is.

> "'For I am the Lord your God. Consecrate yourselves therefore, and be holy, for I am holy. . . . For I am the Lord who brought you up from the land of Egypt to be your God; thus you shall be holy, for I am holy.'" (vv. 44–45)

---

5. Marianne Meye Thompson, *1–3 John*, The IVP New Testament Commentary Series (Downers Grove, Ill.: InterVarsity Press, 1992), p. 43.

Our active involvement is further highlighted in Psalm 24.

> Who may ascend into the hill of the Lord?
> And who may stand in His holy place?
> He who has clean hands and a pure heart,
> Who has not lifted up his soul to falsehood
> And has not sworn deceitfully.
> He shall receive a blessing from the Lord
> And righteousness from the God of his salvation.
> (vv. 3–5; see also Ps. 15; Isa. 58:6–12)

How practical the Lord is! Ethical beauty combined with compassion mark the path to holiness, not withdrawal to monasteries or merciless legalism.

Holiness in the New Testament

What does the New Testament say about how we grow in holiness? First, we need the Cross of Christ to break sin's hold over us (Rom. 6:1–7). Then, because sin still dwells within us—not as a landlord but as a tenant—we must fight the good fight and take action:

> Therefore I urge you, brethren, by the mercies of God, to present your bodies a living and holy sacrifice, acceptable to God, which is your spiritual service of worship. And do not be conformed to this world, but be transformed by the renewing of your mind, so that you may prove what the will of God is, that which is good and acceptable and perfect. (Rom. 12:1–2; see also 6:11–14)

Every day, we must resurrender our lives to the Lord on the altar of His will, committing ourselves to the goal of sanctification:

> For this is the will of God, your sanctification. . . .
> For God has not called us for the purpose of impurity,
> but in sanctification. (1 Thess. 4:3a, 7)

In 1 Peter 1:13–16, we find five practical commands that highlight our part in becoming holy like our Lord:

- first, "prepare your minds for action";

- second, be self-controlled, or "sober in spirit";

- third, "fix your hope completely on the grace . . . of Jesus Christ";

- fourth, "do not be conformed to the former lusts";

- and fifth, in all you do, "be holy" as God is holy (see also 2 Pet. 1:5–7).

Nowhere in these passages do we find the phrase, "Let go and let God." The only letting go we are commanded to do is the letting go of former lusts (1 Pet. 1:14). Throughout Scripture, the Christian life is described as a battle (see Eph. 6:10–18). And there's nothing passive about a soldier in battle. God indeed empowers us (see 2 Pet. 1:4). But we fight the fight (see vv. 5–11; 2 Tim. 4:7).

In Light of What We Have Heard . . .

If we want to stand unashamed in the light of God's holiness, we need to continually do three things. First, we need *to keep ourselves from conforming to former lusts* (1 Pet. 1:14). We need to remember to claim God's power as we lock those things out of our lives. Second, we must *remind ourselves of our calling.* He who has called us is holy, and He has called us to share in that holiness (vv. 15–16; see also 1 Thess. 2:12). Third, we need *to conduct ourselves in fear*, as Peter reveals:

> If you address as Father the One who impartially judges according to each man's work, conduct your-selves in fear during the time of your stay on earth. (1 Pet. 1:17)

This verse doesn't mean fear as in terror but fear as in reverence —an awe-inspiring recognition of God's holiness and purity.

This much of God's will for us is not so mysterious, is it? It's a comfort, a privilege, and a great responsibility.

> You are a chosen race, a royal priesthood, a holy nation, a people for God's own possession, so that you may proclaim the excellencies of Him who has called you out of darkness into His marvelous light. (2:9)

 Living Insights

Having basked in the light of God's holiness, let's take a good, hard look at ourselves. Have we been neglecting the dust when it comes to our own heart's holiness? Have we been indifferent about the cobwebs in the corners of our lives? Are the rugs of our hearts lumpy from years of dirt being swept under them?

The Lord first entered our hearts when they were dusty and disheveled. When He did, He condemned the tenement slums that stood there and consecrated them as temples. Isn't it time for all of us to do some industrial-strength housecleaning?

Which rooms in your spiritual house would you like the Holy Spirit to clean up? Spend a few minutes in prayer, asking the Spirit of God to reveal areas of personal unholiness. Thank God that He loves you anyway, then jot down your discoveries.

_____

_____

_____

_____

_____

_____

Now choose one to focus on this week. Commit it to prayer every morning when you rise. You may even want to write down what you are asking for specifically, leaving some room to record how God answers your prayers.

_____

_____

_____

_____

_____

_____

_____

Don't despair if this messy area isn't spick-and-span overnight; it may be a long-term project. But our holy, righteous Lord never tires of housecleaning.

Questions for Group Discussion

1. Suppose someone describes a friend to you by saying, "He is such a holy person" or "She is the holiest woman I know." What images would the word *holy* conjure up for you?

2. What do you think the Lord means when He commands, "You shall be holy, for I am holy" (1 Pet. 1:16)? How does that command adjust your perception of holiness? How does it guide you personally in your search for God's will?

3. We don't often consider how God's holiness benefits us. Which of the reassurances listed in the lesson means the most to you?

4. In Christ, we stand before God holy and righteous. Which of the privileges of your holy standing means the most to you?

5. As we read in the lesson, "Sanctification is both God's work and our work; a divine promise and a human process." How do you see yourself and God working together to produce holiness in your life? What's your part, and what's God's part?

6. As you close, take some prayerful moments to reflect on the scene in Isaiah 6:1–7. Perhaps someone can read verses 1–4 and pause as group members offer one sentence prayers of praise to our holy God. Read verse 5, then ask the group members to finish Isaiah's words in their hearts: "Woe is me, for I am ruined! Because I am a person of _____." After the group members have had time to reflect, read verses 6–7. Invite the members to offer prayers of gratitude for God's cleansing forgiveness and prayers of commitment to personal holiness.

Chapter 9

SURPRISED BY GOD

Selected Scriptures

I'm pregnant? Oh my . . . how can that be? Well, I mean . . . that *can't* be! Pregnant? Pregnant! You're kidding, right? Ha ha! That's a good one, doctor. Ha ha! You really had me going there . . . OK, joke's over."

This stunned, 45-year-old mother of three had packed up her youngest for college just that week. She and her husband had already begun rearranging their empty nest with long-awaited plans for travel, new hobbies, some rekindled romance. Starting over as parents was *not* in this couple's blueprint for midlife.

Yet there she was, pregnant—she and her husband taken completely by surprise.

Sometimes life takes us by surprise too. We may step forward in what we think is God's plan. Then, abruptly, everything changes. Instead of investing for retirement, we're furnishing a nursery. Instead of looking at a bonus check, we're looking for a new job. Instead of planning a life with a spouse, we're planning dinners for one.

Unexpected changes. Are they really from God? How do we interpret life's surprising and sometimes bewildering turns?

Products of Chance?

Some people say that unexpected events are simply products of chance—part of life running its random course. "God isn't really involved in our daily lives," some believe. "He's more interested in the big picture, the general direction of the world."

Yet, according to His own Word, God rests His hand on the helm of history *and* the details of our days:

> "Does He not see my ways
> And number all my steps?"
> (Job 31:4)

> For the ways of a man are before the eyes of the
> Lord,
> And He watches all his paths.
> (Prov. 5:21)

You scrutinize my path and my lying down,
And are intimately acquainted with all my ways.
(Ps. 139:3)

God's sovereign control extends over us like a canopy. Every life event falls within His plan, even unexpected changes.

Surprises are perhaps the most difficult aspects of God's will to understand, because they defy all our formulas. We kneel before the Lord in prayer. We seek counsel. We read Scripture. We surrender our wills to His. In faith, we move forward . . . only to discover that nothing is like what we thought it would be. It's unfathomable. Beyond understanding. Mysterious.

Surprises in Scripture

We're not the only ones who have been struck by the unpredictability of God's will. Let's take a brief look at three people in Scripture who experienced the unexpected too.

Abraham: A Domestic Crisis

Abram was seventy-five years old when the Lord promised to multiply his descendants into a great nation (see Gen. 12:1–4). Yet this man, whose name means "exalted father," had no children. When God changed his name to Abraham, which means "father of a multitude," he was ninety-nine years old—and *still* no children had been born to him and his wife (chap. 17). The promise of a son at their age seemed laughably impossible (v. 17). Yet, within a year, the most glorious surprise occurred when ninety-year-old Sarah conceived and delivered baby Isaac.

A surprising command. Isaac was the long-awaited branch through which Abraham's family tree would someday grow into a thriving nation—the fulfillment of this father's lifelong dream. So you can imagine the grief that gripped Abraham's heart when God commanded him to cut off the branch before it even had the chance to bud.

> Now it came about after these things, that God tested Abraham, and said to him, "Abraham!" And he said, "Here I am." He said, "Take now your son, your only son, whom you love, Isaac, and go to the land of Moriah, and offer him there as a burnt offering on one of the mountains of which I will tell you." (22:1–2)

How unbelievable, unreasonable, and heartless this command must have seemed. Was God so cruel that He would give an aging man a son only to take him back again? And what about the divine promise that Isaac embodied? Was God taking that back too?

Waiting all those years for Isaac's birth had tested Abraham's faith at one level, but this command tested his faith at the deepest level. Commentator Allen Ross observes,

> It is one thing to claim to trust God's word when waiting for something; it is quite another thing to trust and obey His word after [that something] is received. This was a test of how much Abraham would obey God's word. Would he cling to the boy now that he had him, or would he still obey and return him to the Lord? In other words how far would Abraham go in obedience? Did he really believe that God would still keep His word and raise the seed of promise?[1]

An unexpected grace. Was Abraham's faith stronger than his paternal instincts? His actions show the answer. Bundling some wood, he rose early the next morning and took Isaac on a three-day journey to the mountain of God. There he built an altar, bound his son, and laid him on it (see vv. 3–9). Fully intending to obey God's command, he stretched his hand over Isaac, the knife poised and ready to plunge (v. 10). Suddenly, God surprised Abraham again, this time with a poignant display of grace.

> But the angel of the Lord called to him from heaven and said, "Abraham, Abraham!" And he said, "Here I am." He said, "Do not stretch out your hand against the lad, and do nothing to him; for now I know that you fear God, since you have not withheld your son, your only son, from Me." Then Abraham raised his eyes and looked, and behold, behind him a ram caught in the thicket by his horns; and Abraham went and took the ram and offered him up for a burnt offering in the place of his son. (vv. 11–13)

---

1. Allen P. Ross, "Genesis," in *The Bible Knowledge Commentary*, Old Testament edition, ed. John F. Walvoord and Roy B. Zuck (Colorado Springs, Colo.: Chariot Victor Publishing, 1985), p. 64.

In the surprising plan of God, Abraham received a son with joy and released him in faith, only to receive him back again. Sometimes the surprises of God present our families with similar domestic crises. How will we respond when our faith is tested? Can we let go of the people and the things we love when the unexpected happens?

Joseph: A Lifestyle Crisis

Abraham's dreams of a son came true in Isaac, who had a son, Jacob, who had a son, Joseph, who had dreams of a different sort come true. Joseph's first dream revealed his older brothers bowing to him as their ruler (Gen. 37:6–8); in the second, his father and mother joined his brothers in reverent submission (vv. 9–10). In this strictly hierarchical culture, authority was passed from father to sons in order of birth. The idea that Jacob's eleventh son, Joseph, would rule his family was as implausible as a mailroom clerk being promoted to CEO. Yet in the surprising will of God, that kind of promotion was Joseph's destiny.

Bewildering trials. Even more surprising, though, was the unlikely training program God had in store for this ruler-to-be. Most young princes in Joseph's day were tutored by the greatest minds, treated to the finest privileges, and sheltered in the richest palaces. Joseph was sold as a slave, falsely convicted of rape, and locked away in an Egyptian dungeon (chaps. 37, 39).

This dizzying downward spiral must have made Joseph's mind spin with questions. His brothers had rejected him; his friends had forgotten him. Had God forsaken him too? Hardly! Two years later, when Pharaoh had a disturbing nightmare, the royal cupbearer told him about a certain Hebrew dream-teller he had met in prison. The king summoned Joseph, who promptly interpreted his dream: seven years of plenty would be followed by seven years of famine (40:1–41:37).

Joseph's strange journey had begun with his own dreams; now the dream of another had brought it to completion. Pharaoh appointed Joseph as prime minister, in charge of gathering grain and preparing the nation for the impending famine (41:38–49).

Unforeseen reunion. But God's plan included more surprises. Among the famine refugees who poured into Egypt searching for food were Joseph's brothers. When the prime minister revealed his true identity, his brothers trembled with fear (42:1–45:3). Would their spurned-brother-now-ruler take revenge for the years of hardship they caused him? Having learned to rest in God's surprises, Joseph expressed to his brothers a heavenly perspective on his pain:

"God sent me before you to preserve for you a remnant in the earth, and to keep you alive by a great deliverance. Now, therefore, it was not you who sent me here, but God." (45:7–8a)

The betrayal, the injustice, the broken promises—God was working through them all. Later, Joseph consoled his fearful brothers again with this hallmark principle of the life of faith:

"As for you, *you meant evil against me, but God meant it for good* in order to bring about this present result, to preserve many people alive." (50:20, emphasis added)

Can God redeem our lifestyle crises? Can He work others' evils for our good? Thankfully, yes. In our own dungeon experiences, we can find hope in that heavenly perspective.

David: A Career Crisis

Like Joseph, David was a youth when God revealed His will for his life. The anointing oil that poured from Samuel's flask onto David's thick hair and down his smooth cheeks signified that this shepherd boy was God's choice for the next king of Israel. God's selection of Jesse's youngest son was only the beginning of the surprises He had in store for David (1 Sam. 16:1–13).

Heroic deed, jealous king. David's first test of faith was the towering Goliath, whom David defeated with courageous faith and a swing of his deadly sling (chap. 17). This heroic deed put David on the road to the crown, but it was not the smooth journey he might have expected. While the victory over Goliath moved David into the national spotlight, it also exposed him to the vindictive jealousy of King Saul. As David's star rose higher and higher, so did the temperature of Saul's blood. Finally, the king exploded in rage and hurled his spear at David, intending to pin the young hero to the wall next to his latest hunting trophy. Fortunately, the spear missed its target, and David escaped unharmed (18:1–11).

Painful journey. That narrow escape from Saul's murderous hand would be the first of many over the course of the next decade or so as David fled from rock to cave throughout the Judean wilderness (chaps. 19–30). In God's surprising will, David's most fearsome giant was not the rumbling Goliath but his own king and countryman, Saul. And his road to the crown led him not along smooth paths of honor but rocky trails of mistreatment and pain.

Patience and integrity. After years of waiting, David finally fulfilled his anointing when Saul died. He first became king of Judah in Hebron, then king of all Israel in Jerusalem (1 Sam. 31:1–2 Sam. 5:12). David's experience with the unexpected teaches us the importance of patience and integrity—two traits that are particularly needed in a career crisis. A jealous king will never hound us through the wilderness, but we might feel an angry boss breathing down our necks. And we might endure a long delay in a promised promotion or a sudden shift of corporate favor. From David's life, we learn that these sorts of trials are part of God's surprising will to prepare us for something we can't yet see. Even though it's not the path we would choose, we can rest knowing our Shepherd is leading us through.

Four Concluding Principles

What can we conclude from these examples? First, *God's preferred method is surprise.* Knowing that God tests our faith with unexpected changes keeps us from being too alarmed when they come.

Second, *His surprises require flexibility and adaptability.* We must be willing to follow Plan B when God scratches out our Plan A.

Third, *behind God's surprises are purposes we are not aware of.* Rather than become angry and try to pin blame when the unexpected happens, remind yourself that this is no mistake. God has a plan. What can you learn about Him and yourself through this turn of events?

Finally, *when God surprises us, He supplies sufficient grace to handle the unexpected.* He supplied a lamb when Abraham released his son; He honored Joseph when he endured mistreatment; He protected David when he kept his integrity. His hand of grace is outstretched toward us as well, perhaps not to alter our circumstances but to minister to us through them as we learn to embrace His surprising will.

Living Insights

By definition, a *surprise* is something unexpected. If we expect a surprise, it won't be a surprise, will it? Some people spend their lives trying to anticipate the changes lurking around the corner. And when a surprise blindsides them (as it most assuredly will), they berate themselves for not having seen it coming. They blame themselves for not being smarter or more perceptive or a better judge of character.

Although self-blame is a natural tendency after an unexpected car accident, for example, or a job loss or family tragedy, it does us no good. Blaming others doesn't help matters either, and neither does blaming God. What can we do when the unexpected happens?

What did Abraham, Joseph, and David do when they were blindsided by the unexpected?

_____

_____

_____

_____

What direction does their response to surprises give you in your situation?

_____

_____

_____

_____

In his book *The Mystery of God's Will*, Chuck offers this concluding encouragement:

> Wherever you are in this journey called life, wherever you may be employed, wherever you may be in your domestic situation, wherever you may be in your age, your health, or your lifestyle, God may be preparing you for a great surprise in order to find you faithful. Rather than running from Him, let me suggest the opposite: Run *toward* Him. And rather than looking for someone to blame for the pain that you're now enduring or the change that's on the horizon, look heavenward and realize that this arrangement is sovereignly put together for your good and for His glory.[2]

2. Charles R. Swindoll, *The Mystery of God's Will* (Nashville, Tenn.: Word Publishing, 1999), p. 181.

Questions for Group Discussion

1. Along the timeline of your life, what major events stand out as surprises or unexpected changes? Describe some of your reactions: perhaps fear, anger, blame, or panic. What else?

2. When the unexpected happened to you, was God calling you to:
   a. release something or someone you loved, like Abraham,
   b. accept and endure mistreatment, like Joseph,
   c. wait patiently for something promised, like David, or
   d. demonstrate some other act of faith?

3. During your trial, what did you learn about God? About yourself?

4. What advice would you give yourself if (or when) the unexpected happens again?

Chapter 10

CLOSED DOORS, OPEN DOORS

Revelation 3:7–8; Acts 15:40–16:14

A slammed door makes a harsh sound, doesn't it? It's harsh to the ears and the heart. It rings of rejection, refusal, and exclusion. And it's so absolute, like the exclamation point on a sign that says, "No Trespassing!" or "Keep Out!"

A blocked opportunity can seem like a slammed door. After much prayer and wise counsel, you expectantly set out for a particular goal that you feel certain is God's will. The road is smooth and the timing seems right, then, without warning—slam! The university you hoped to attend rejects your admission request. The relationship you thought might lead to marriage ends in a breakup. The house you had your heart set on is sold to another family. The contract you worked months to win is awarded to another firm. You may ask yourself, "Why did things not turn out as planned? What did I do wrong?"

Perhaps it's not a matter of doing wrong. Although the closed door feels like a rebuff, it may be an unexpected blessing. Behind that closed door may be a hand of grace.

The One Who Opens and Shuts

In Revelation 3:7b, John records Jesus' words to the church in ancient Philadelphia—words that may shed some light on our closed-door experiences:

> "He who is holy, who is true, who has the key of David, who opens and no one will shut, and who shuts and no one opens."

Jesus is the subject here. He is holy—completely pure in all His motives and actions. He is true—thoroughly reliable, dependable.

Portions of this chapter have been adapted from "What Opens When Doors Close?" from the study guide *The Growth of an Expanding Mission*, coauthored by Bryce Klabunde, from the Bible-teaching ministry of Charles R. Swindoll (Anaheim, Calif.: Insight for Living, 1992), pp. 132–40.

And He has the "key of David"—the messianic authority to open and shut the kingdom of God to whomever He chooses.

This verse assures us that Jesus alone (not Satan or any earthly power) has final authority over our eternal destiny. He holds the key to the door of heaven . . . and all the other doors in our lives as well.

We are more used to thinking of Christ as a door opener, not the door closer, aren't we? But He does both. He is the One who opens and shuts, and His reasons are always holy and true.

Paul's Open and Closed Door Experiences

The apostle Paul discovered both sides of God's will during His second missionary journey. Let's follow him on a portion of this trip and see how our trustworthy Lord guided him through.

Preparations for the Second Journey

Paul's first missionary journey was a great success, producing many Gentile converts and new churches. Upon returning home, Paul and his companion, Barnabas, reported to the Antioch church "all things that God had done with them and how He had opened a door of faith to the Gentiles" (Acts 14:27). Surely, God would hold this door of faith open on Paul's second trip too.

In addition, the Jerusalem Council had recently laid the doctrinal foundation for Gentile salvation (15:6–29). The only glitch Paul had experienced was a falling out with his old friend Barnabas about whether to take young John Mark with them on their next journey. Barnabas wanted to bring him; Paul did not (vv. 36–39). So Paul found a new traveling partner, Silas, and departed with the full support and encouragement of the Antioch church (v. 40).

Blessings in Familiar Territory

Intending to pick up where Paul left off on his first journey and carry the gospel deeper into Asia, he and Silas hiked to Tarsus, Paul's hometown, through a pass called the Cilician Gates, and up into the Taurus Mountains. This was familiar territory for Paul, a welcome sight as he walked along, savoring the anticipation of reunion with his Galatian friends.

Strengthening the churches. Paul and Silas first met with churches in Syria and Cilicia, where the doors were wide open for them to accomplish their first objective: to strengthen the churches (15:41). Luke, the author of Acts, records no persecution so far on this journey, unlike Paul's first trip, where he suffered much abuse. Instead, he and Silas were free to teach and encourage the Christians.

Choosing Timothy. When they came to Derbe and then Lystra, one of Paul's young converts, Timothy, impressed them with his rapid growth in Christ. Here is the first mention of this man who would become Paul's protégé and one of the early church's first pastors (16:1–3).

What the Apostle had seen lacking in John Mark (who deserted him on his first journey, see 15:38), he found in Timothy. This young man had a good reputation among the believers in the area and was willing to stay by his side on the road. This was another open door for Paul—he longed to prepare a younger man to carry on the ministry, and Timothy was the perfect choice.[1]

Delivering decrees. With Timothy aboard, the missionaries traveled throughout the region explaining the decree from the Jerusalem Council (16:4). The churches were "being strengthened in the faith," Luke tells us (v. 5a), which shows yet another open door in their ministry.

Experiencing growth. Luke also records encouraging, phenomenal growth in every church.

> The churches . . . were increasing in number daily.
> (v. 5b)

With the believers' numbers continually multiplying, the missionaries must have felt a fresh spring in their step and a fire in their souls. At every turn, the wind of God's Spirit was pushing doors open for the gospel. Surely, as the three men ventured further into Asia, God would whisk them through more open doors to even greater successes! Hearts pounding with anticipation, they headed into the surrounding regions. Suddenly, though, the wind stopped.

Blocked from New Regions

> They passed through the Phrygian and Galatian region, having been forbidden by the Holy Spirit to speak the word in Asia. (v. 6)

---

1. Because Timothy was half-Jewish—his mother was a Jewish believer, but his father was Greek—Paul circumcised him to remove any barriers to Jews accepting the gospel. This way the Jews could not say, "We're not interested" because of Timothy, and the new Jewish believers would not be turned off to Timothy as a pastor in training.

As Paul, Silas, and Timothy tried to forge ahead, the Holy Spirit shut fast the door of opportunity. Perhaps they were prohibited from preaching or they were met with cool rejection. Or maybe they sensed in their spirit a telling uneasiness. Whatever they experienced, they took it as a sign from the Spirit. So they went another way, but the doors closed again. Like mice in a maze, they wandered from here to there, not able to settle or minister anywhere in Phrygia or Galatia.

Eventually, they arrived at the outskirts of the next province.

> And after they came to Mysia, they were trying to go into Bithynia, and the Spirit of Jesus did not permit them; and passing by Mysia, they came down to Troas. (vv. 7–8)

More closed doors! Try as they may, God was blocking their efforts. Was it for lack of needy people in these regions? On the contrary, these men and women needed Christ too. Even so, Christ was restraining His messengers and His message.

Likewise, in our lives, God will sometimes shut down an exciting ministry or allow obstacles in our paths like sickness, financial difficulties, job loss, or a broken relationship. At times like these, it's easy to become frustrated and disheartened. We can't imagine why God would shut some of the doors that He does. So we try to explain it, saying, "Maybe we just made a mistake . . . maybe we need to try harder." And we jiggle the doorknobs, test the locks, rap on the door, but it is closed tight.

When Christ shuts a door, though, He usually has His sights on something better—something around the bend we can't see yet. For Paul, that something was Europe.

Directed to Another Plan

Paul had planned to evangelize Asia, but for now, Asia was merely God's hallway for His men to pass through.

A vision. The very end of the corridor was Troas, a city on the western edge of Asia that overlooked the Aegean Sea (v. 8). God had blocked them from going north, south, or east; so here they stood with their toes in the sand, at Asia's westernmost point. Who would they witness to here? The fish?

There was nothing to do except wait on God and get some rest. We don't know how many days or weeks they waited in Troas, but one night, while they slept,

A vision appeared to Paul in the night: a man of Macedonia was standing and appealing to him, and saying, "Come over to Macedonia and help us." (v. 9)

"That's it!" Paul must have thought. God had opened the one remaining door. Across the sea was Macedonia, a region that is part of modern-day Greece. Had Paul, in frustration, returned to Antioch earlier or stubbornly resisted the Holy Spirit's barricades in Asia, he would have missed this opportunity. Finally, the time of testing and waiting was over, and the missionaries could get to the business of evangelism.

A person. Right away, they made preparations to cross over to Macedonia. But before leaving Troas, they added a fourth man to the team. Notice who this person is from the pronoun Luke uses in verse 10.

When [Paul] had seen the vision, immediately *we* sought to go into Macedonia, concluding that God had called *us* to preach the gospel to them. (v. 10, emphasis added)

It's Luke himself.[2] Possibly a citizen of Troas, Dr. Luke perhaps joined the mission as Paul's physician, perhaps, but definitely as an evangelist in his own right. Again, the closed doors in Asia were a blessing, because if it hadn't been for them, Paul might have missed meeting Luke.

Luke notes a significant point: "God had *called* us to preach the gospel" to the Macedonian people (v. 10b, emphasis added). The missionaries hadn't sensed that calling for Asia, in spite of the ever-present needs around them. Christ was pointing them onward to Troas, where they could receive this call to Europe. Now they could press forward confidently, knowing Christ had opened the door and was with them all the way.

A divine meeting. Luke documents the first experience of evangelism in Europe.

So putting out to sea from Troas, we ran a straight course to Samothrace, and on the day following to Neapolis; and from there to Philippi, which is a

---

2. There are three "we" sections in Acts in which Luke accompanies Paul personally: 16:10–17; 20:5–21:18; and 27:1–28:16.

leading city of the district of Macedonia, a Roman colony; and we were staying in this city for some days. And on the Sabbath day we went outside the gate to a riverside, where we were supposing that there would be a place of prayer; and we sat down and began speaking to the women who had assembled. A woman named Lydia, from the city of Thyatira, a seller of purple fabrics, a worshiper of God, was listening; and the Lord opened her heart to respond to the things spoken by Paul. (vv. 11–14)

Just think, Lydia was the reason Paul and his companions had come this far. This one woman. And if she had been the only convert, their frustrating, tortuous journey would have been worthwhile. Lydia was the first European Christian, but in God's perfect plan, she was not the last. Many more would embrace the gospel in the continent of Europe, all the way to Rome and beyond.

Message Applied

Are you searching for God's call and finding nothing but closed doors? Whether they come in the form of sickness, failure, or frustrating circumstances, Paul's story offers four truths that will give you hope.

First, because God is sovereign, He is in full control—even of blocked opportunities. *Second,* God takes full responsibility for whatever results from a closed door—let Him carry the burden. *Third,* the closing of a good opportunity often occurs in order to lead us to a better one. Recall the psalmist's words:

No good thing does He withhold from those who
walk uprightly. (Ps. 84:11b)

And Jesus' words too:

"If you then, being evil, know how to give good gifts
to your children, how much more will your Father
who is in heaven give what is good to those who
ask Him!" (Matt. 7:11)

And *fourth,* not until we walk through the open door will we realize the necessity of the closed ones. Stopping the journey because of a disappointing "no" may cause you to miss the joy of a future "yes." Keep moving forward until you reach the open door. Then the mystery will be made clear.

Living Insights

Paul was seeking Asia when God opened Europe.

We may be seeking a certain school or career, relationship or ministry—only to have God open a door to a future far better than we imagined. This delightful, unexpected turn of events is called a _serendipity_.

Webster's defines the word simply as "the faculty or phenomenon of finding valuable or agreeable things not sought for."[3] The path of God's will is full of serendipitous opportunities. Experiencing them depends on our willingness to abandon our failed goal, grasp the unexpected, and respond to a new opportunity. Stubbornly pounding on closed doors is a surefire way to miss God's serendipities.

If God unexpectedly opened a door in your life, would you be free enough to enter it? Or are you so bound up by the disappointment of a closed door that you couldn't move?

Could God be offering you a serendipity right now? Could He be opening a door you hadn't planned on? How can you alter your course to abandon the closed door and enter the open one?

---

3. _Merriam-Webster's Collegiate Dictionary_, 10th ed., see "serendipity."

Questions for Group Discussion

1. Closed doors are often accompanied by feelings of deep disappointment, failure, frustration, rejection, anger, confusion, and fear. Which emotion have you felt the strongest during your closed-door experiences?

2. Can you identify some of Paul's possible emotions as he and his companions met closed doors in Asia? What fears might he have struggled with? Would you have pressed on?

3. John Stott offers some suggestions for how Paul and his companions were stopped by the Holy Spirit from ministering in Asia: "It may have been through giving the missionaries a strong, united inward impression, or through some outward circumstance like illness, Jewish opposition or a legal ban, or through the utterance of a Christian prophet, perhaps Silas himself (15:32)."[4] How have you known that God was closing a door in your life?

4. "When God closes a door, He opens a window." That saying has been around a long time. Is it just wishful thinking, or have you found it to be true?

5. In Paul's case, the "window" was Lydia. Her conversion was just as significant in God's program as the conversion of three thousand on the Day of Pentecost (see Acts 2:37–41). Sometimes we can let our disappointment over a big, closed opportunity blind us to the small but significant window that God has opened. What are some small God-opportunities you may have overlooked until now? What can you do this week to explore them?

4. John Stott, *The Spirit, the Church, and the World: The Message of Acts* (Downers Grove, Ill.: InterVarsity Press, 1990), p. 260.

Chapter 11

A BETTER WAY TO LOOK AT GOD'S WILL

Job 23:1–17; Romans 8:25–30

Looking back on our study, we've examined some of the hard mysteries of God's will:

> unexpected turns,
> closed opportunities,
> agonizing delays,
> unanswered prayers,
> confusing periods of silence.

The experience of these mysteries often feels like stumbling through a thick fog—twisting our ankles in unseen holes, bruising our shins on hidden rocks. Yet in the midst of this buffeting comes God's outstretched hand of blessing, offering His mercy, faithfulness, and holiness to comfort and to guide. His Word reassures us that someday He will lift all the mysteries that shroud our lives. In his paraphrase of Paul's words from 1 Corinthians 13:12, Eugene Peterson pictures that day:

> We don't yet see things clearly. We're squinting in a fog, peering through a mist. But it won't be long before the weather clears and the sun shines bright! We'll see it all then, see it all as clearly as God sees us, knowing him directly just as he knows us![1]

What a sunburst that will be! Until that happy day, though, we'll still stumble and squint, struggling to make sense of things. We may reduce the number of bruises, however, by readjusting our perspective toward God's will and His mysteries.

Two Possible Perspectives

How we interpret and feel about God's will often depends on

---

1. Eugene H. Peterson, *The Message: The New Testament in Contemporary English* (Colorado Springs, Colo.: NavPress, 1993), p. 360.

our point of view. We can choose between two possible perspectives: the human and the divine.

Through Human Eyes

Our natural choice is to see things from a human point of view—after all, we are human. The problem with this perspective is that we are inherently self-centered. We are born viewing the world as a place for getting our needs and wishes met. As we mature, our perspective broadens, but we still tend to perceive ourselves at the center of everything. It's as if we look at life through mirrored sunglasses that are reversed—we see every life event as it reflects on us, and we project our interests and ways of thinking onto others.

When we view God through human eyes, we see Him like us, perhaps stronger and wiser, but essentially with the same human values. Consequently, when He acts in ways that are different from ours, we judge Him as unfair or untrustworthy. We evaluate Him by our standards. Our faith shatters when bad things happen to innocent people. How could God do such a thing? If *we* were God, we would never allow hurricanes to destroy homes or good people to die young.

Humanly speaking, God's will is illogical sometimes. It doesn't make sense *to us*. To God, of course, it makes perfect sense. His will is no mystery to Him! That's why we need to try to see the events of life not through human eyes but through God's eyes.

Through God's Eyes

Seeing through God's eyes requires us to think theologically. Thinking theologically means *using the truth of Scripture as our primary guide for interpreting life*. For example, difficult circumstances may lead us to believe that God does not care about us. However, Scripture assures us of God's love and reveals Jesus' death on our behalf as the supreme demonstration of His love (see Rom. 5:8). We know that God is working all the events of our lives together for our good and His ultimate glory (8:28–29). Knowing these truths helps us trust Him and rest in His will.

Theological thinking places God at the center. It helps us focus on His purposes, His desires, and His glory rather than our needs, our problems, and our happiness. The psalmist tells us the emotional benefits of this God-centered mind-set:

> Those who love Your law have great peace,
> And nothing causes them to stumble. (Ps. 119:165)

Thinking theologically gives us peace of mind. But it requires faith—believing what we do know about God and trusting Him with what we don't know (see Heb. 11:1). There are worlds of knowledge beyond the borders of our human experience that only God sees. If we want to seek God's perspective, we must be willing to admit that these worlds exist, even though we can't see them. And that takes faith.

We must also humbly admit that our understanding of what is right and wrong, fair and unfair, is skewed by our limited knowledge. We can't see the overall picture, so how do we know for certain what is best? God knows the beginning from the end; as the psalmist writes, "His understanding is infinite" (Ps. 147:5b). *Infinite* means "immeasurably or inconceivably great . . . inexhaustible."[2]

Out of His limitless range of knowledge, God sets the course of our days. It's no surprise, then, that we can't always explain His will. Proverbs acknowledges our limitation:

Man's steps are ordained by the Lord,
How then can man understand his way? (20:24)

Since God is unsearchable and beyond comprehension (see Rom. 11:33–34), how can we begin to understand His will? It's too deep to fathom and too profound to explain.

The challenge for us, then, is not to figure out the mysteries of God and of life—even though we desperately want explanations—but to learn to rest in and know better God Himself. As Jeremiah recorded:

Thus says the Lord, "Let not a wise man boast of his wisdom, and let not the mighty man boast of his might, let not a rich man boast of his riches; but let him who boasts boast of this, that he understands and knows Me, that I am the Lord who exercises loving-kindness, justice and righteousness on earth; for I delight in these things," declares the Lord. (Jer. 9:23–24)

Job: A Man Who Learned to See through God's Eyes

The book of Job is the story of a man who learned to see through God's eyes and, eventually, find rest. His is a painful story, filled

2. *Merriam-Webster's Collegiate Dictionary*, 10th ed., see "infinite."

89

with confusion and anger, but he has much to teach us.[3]

Job's Predicament

If you recall, Job lost everything dear to him: his livelihood, his possessions, his servants, and his children (Job 1:13–19). He even lost his health, stricken by Satan with "sore boils from the sole of his foot to the crown of his head" (2:7). Crushed physically and devastated emotionally, poor Job could only shake his head in bewilderment, wondering why such tragedies would happen to one who had followed God faithfully and blamelessly (see 1:1). Still,

> Through all this Job did not sin nor did he blame God. (v. 22)

Several of his friends came to console him, but their words of comfort soon turned to heavy-handed advice. Feeling shut off from God, misunderstood and attacked by his so-called counselors, and lost in an endless tunnel of troubles, Job uttered a heartfelt "if only."

Job's Desire

> Then Job replied,
> "Even today my complaint is rebellion;
> His hand is heavy despite my groaning.
> Oh that I knew where I might find Him,
> That I might come to His seat!
> I would present my case before Him
> And fill my mouth with arguments.
> I would learn the words which He would answer,
> And perceive what He would say to me.
> Would He contend with me by the greatness of
> His power?
> No, surely He would pay attention to me.
> There the upright would reason with Him;
> And I would be delivered forever from my Judge."
> (23:1–7)

Job longed to meet face-to-face with God, to get a chance to argue his side of things at a fair trial. He knew he hadn't done anything

---

3. This section has been adapted from the study guide *What It Takes to Win*, coauthored by Bryce Klabunde, from the Bible-teaching ministry of Charles R. Swindoll (1993; reprint, Anaheim, Calif.: Insight for Living, 1999), pp. 90–94.

to deserve the calamities that were ravaging his life, and he believed that God, who is just and righteous, would agree with him and set things right. But Job couldn't seem to find Him (v. 3).

And as he reeled around looking everywhere for God, Job's heart churned with frustration.

> "Behold, I go forward but He is not there,
> And backward, but I cannot perceive Him;
> When He acts on the left, I cannot behold Him;
> He turns on the right, I cannot see Him."
> (vv. 8–9)

All he perceived was the trial in this life—God grinding and pounding him in a painful ordeal.

Job's Consolation

That's all he could see—except for a brief moment when he could get his head above his pain and think theologically. Job then remembered three reassuring truths about his sovereign Judge.

God knows me. In contrast to his frustrated efforts to find God, Job could rest in the fact that God knew where he was:

> "But He knows the way I take; . . .
> My foot has held fast to His path;
> I have kept His way and not turned aside.
> I have not departed from the command of His lips;
> I have treasured the words of His mouth more
>   than my necessary food." (vv. 10a, 11–12)

God knew Job's character because God's ways were Job's well-worn path. Job had not departed from God's commandments and had treasured His words (vv. 11–12).

There's a comfort in knowing that God knows us, isn't there? God knows us inside and out, up and down, coming and going (see Ps. 139:1–3). He watches over us for our benefit, shaping our character with our best interests in mind.

God refines me. Because God knew the integrity of his ways, Job next asserted,

> "When He has tried me, I shall come forth as gold."
> (Job 23:10b)

Job was confident that his trials would eventually reveal his golden character. Not many of us can lay claim to such a twenty-four-karat nature, can we? One of the purposes of our trials is to serve as refining fires, burning off our sinful dross to form hearts of pure gold.

In the midst of the fire, we do well to remember that God is more interested in perfecting our ways than explaining His. There is a purpose to His mysteries—a larger plan that is not necessarily designed to make us comfortable, but one that is designed to make us Christlike.

As Paul wrote, God's intention since the beginning has been to draw all things together in Christ:

> In all wisdom and insight He made known to us the mystery of His will, according to His kind intention which He purposed in Him with a view to an administration suitable to the fullness of the times, that is, *the summing up of all things in Christ*, things in the heavens and things on the earth. (Eph. 1:8b–10, emphasis added)

What can we do while awaiting this glorious moment of the culmination of all things in Christ? In Romans, Paul says that we must persevere (Rom. 8:25). To help us in the midst of our groaning (v. 23), God's Spirit intercedes for us with sympathetic groanings of His own (vv. 26–27). And God reassures us that He is working all things according to His good and sovereign purpose (v. 28). The goal of all this is our conformity to the image of Christ and our ultimate glorification in Him (vv. 29–30). What a wonderful hope we have!

God hears me. The hope of glory eases our minds, but what about the daily pain? Job knew that his pain was still ever present and that the end didn't soften the means.

> "But He is unique and who can turn Him?
> And what His soul desires, that He does.
> For He performs what is appointed for me,
> And many such decrees are with Him.
> Therefore, I would be dismayed at His presence;
> When I consider, I am terrified of Him.
> It is God who has made my heart faint,
> And the Almighty who has dismayed me,
> But I am not silenced by the darkness,
> Nor deep gloom which covers me."
> (Job 23:13–17)

Although Job trembled in the shadow of God's sovereign hand, he was "not silenced by the darkness." He would keep speaking, keep puzzling out his situation and crying to God. And so can we.

A Better Way to See

So, in a nutshell, the better way to see the will of God is this: *God's will is God's way of shaping us into the image of Christ.* God's will may involve moving us from one job to the next or one state to the next. It may involve which house we live in and what kind of car we drive. It may involve where we go to school, whom we marry, and how many children we have. However, as much as we like to focus on these major life issues, God's will is primarily about the larger issue of maturity in Christ.

When you find yourself in the midst of one of God's mysteries, then, keep in mind these four points, which are based on Romans 8:25–30.

First, *wait and persevere.* Don't panic. Don't doubt God's love. Don't give up hope.

Second, *face the test on your knees.* It's OK to express your emotions to the Lord. He has provided the Spirit, who groans along with you, to lift your burdens in prayer.

Third, *rest in the sovereign God and His plan.* You won't be able to figure out the plan, so don't try. Instead, focus your mind on the truths of Scripture and surrender yourself to Him.

Fourth, *let God conform you to the image of Christ.* Spend less time analyzing God and more time obeying Him. Be sensitive to the lessons He is teaching you during the misty, mysterious seasons of life.

And be encouraged. It won't be long before the weather clears.

 Living Insights

It's not easy to admit our inability to understand God's ways. We want knowledge. We want explanations. We want to be able to reason things out. That certainly was Job's desire. He desperately wanted to understand why God was allowing his afflictions. They didn't make sense to him, and he believed he had a legitimate complaint before God.

We may believe that we have legitimate complaints too. It's not fair that our cheating coworker got the promotion we deserved.

It's not fair that the car accident robbed us of our dear child, and the drunk driver who hit us walked away with hardly a scratch. It's not fair that our spouse sunk into a lifestyle of sin and destroyed the family.

Based on what we know, we are probably right; however, we don't know everything. Our perception of what is right and fair is limited to the few threads we can see. God views the entire tapestry and bases His will for us on His understanding—which is infinite, immeasurable, and incomprehensible.

Our only response is to surrender to the Weaver's hand and let go of our unanswered questions. Call it what it is, an unsolvable mystery—and let it be.

If you've been wrestling with God over recent puzzling events, perhaps it would help to remind yourself of His unfathomable nature. Review the verses we quoted at the beginning of this study guide—Job 11:7–9; Isaiah 55:8–9; Romans 11:33–36. You may wish to use the space below to release your complaints to Him.

_____

_____

_____

_____

_____

_____

_____

_____

_____

_____

_____

_____

And the peace of God, which surpasses all comprehension, will guard your hearts and your minds in Christ Jesus. (Phil. 4:7)

Questions for Group Discussion

We began our study of the mystery of God's will by proposing that knowing His will is more than making good decisions and getting from point A to point B. It's about the journey itself and who we are becoming along the way. In his book *The Mystery of God's Will*, Chuck Swindoll draws this idea to a conclusion:

> The overarching will of God is not about geography. (Where should I go?) It is not about occupation. (Where should I work?) It is not about exactly what car I should drive. (What color do you prefer?) The overarching, big-picture will of God is not centered in the petty details of everyday life that we worry over. The will of God is primarily and ultimately concerned about our becoming like Christ. And in that sense, the will of God is a test. When He's tried us, and we have responded in obedience (even though we didn't understand why), we will come forth as gold.[4]

1. What's your opinion of Chuck's conclusion? In what ways does it impact your understanding of God's will?

2. Have you experienced God's will as a test? How so?

3. Would you say that you have been looking at your present situation through human eyes or God's eyes?

4. What advantage is there to "thinking theologically"? How might it alter your present point of view?

5. What's one new insight from this study that you can wrap up and take with you on your journey? As the group closes in prayer, take a moment to meditate on Eugene Peterson's paraphrase of 1 Corinthians 13:12 that we quoted in this chapter's introduction. Offer prayers of thanksgiving for the hope this verse gives.

---

4. Charles R. Swindoll, *The Mystery of God's Will: What Does He Want for Me?* (Nashville, Tenn.: Word Publishing, 1999), p. 207.

BOOKS FOR
PROBING FURTHER

The more we discover about God's will, the more we realize there is to discover. It is a never-ending journey—one that we encourage you to continue through these suggested resources. May they lead you to an even greater appreciation for the mysteries of God's will.

Dobson, James. *When God Doesn't Make Sense*. Wheaton, Ill.: Tyndale House Publishers, 1993.

Fee, Gordon D., and Douglas Stuart. *How to Read the Bible for All Its Worth: A Guide to Understanding the Bible*. Grand Rapids, Mich.: Zondervan Publishing House, Academie Books, 1982.

Hendricks, Howard G., and William D. Hendricks. *Living by the Book*. Chicago, Ill.: Moody Press, 1991.

Howard, J. Grant, Jr. *Knowing God's Will—and Doing It!* Grand Rapids, Mich.: Zondervan Publishing House, 1976.

Kreeft, Peter. *Making Sense Out of Suffering*. Ann Arbor, Mich.: Servant Books, 1986.

Kuhatschek, Jack. *Taking the Guesswork out of Applying the Bible*. Downers Grove, Ill.: InterVarsity Press, 1990.

Waltke, Bruce. *Knowing the Will of God*. Eugene, Ore.: Harvest House Publishers, 1998.

Willard, Dallas. *Hearing God: Developing a Conversational Relationship with God*. Downers Grove, Ill.: InterVarsity Press, 1999.

Some of these books may be out of print and available only through a library. For those currently available, please contact your local Christian bookstore. Books by Charles R. Swindoll, as well as some books by other authors, may be obtained through Insight for Living.

Insight for Living also offers study guides on many books of the Bible, as well as on a variety of issues and biblical personalities. For more information, see the ordering instructions that follow and contact the office that serves you.

ORDERING INFORMATION

THE MYSTERY OF GOD'S WILL

If you would like to order additional study guides, purchase the cassette series that accompanies this guide, or request our product catalogs, please contact the office that serves you.

United States and International locations:
Insight for Living
Post Office Box 69000
Anaheim, CA 92817-0900

1-800-772-8888, 24 hours a day, seven days a week
(714) 575-5000, 8:00 A.M. to 4:30 P.M., Pacific time, Monday to Friday

Canada:
Insight for Living Ministries
Post Office Box 2510
Vancouver, BC, Canada V6B 3W7

1-800-663-7639, 24 hours a day, seven days a week

Australia:
Insight for Living, Inc.
General Post Office Box 2823 EE
Melbourne, VIC 3001, Australia

Toll-free 1800-772-888 or (03) 9877-4277, 8·30 A M to 5·00 P.M., Monday to Friday

World Wide Web:
www.insight.org

Study Guide Subscription Program

Study guide subscriptions are available. Please call or write the office nearest you to find out how you can receive our study guides on a regular basis.